THAT
PALE
MOTHER
RISING

THAT PALE MOTHER RISING

Sentimental Discourses and the
Imitation of Motherhood in
19th-Century America

Eva Cherniavsky

Indiana University Press
Bloomington • Indianapolis

The paper used in this publication meets the minimum requirements of
American National Standard for Information Sciences—Permanence of
Paper for Printed Materials, ANSI Z39.48-1984.

Library of Congress Cataloging-in-Publication Data

Cherniavsky, Eva, date
   That pale mother rising : sentimental discourses and the
imitation of motherhood in nineteenth–century America /
Eva Cherniavsky.
      p.   cm.
   Includes bibliographical references and index.
   ISBN 0-253-31343-0. —ISBN 0-253-20934-X (pbk.)
   1. Feminist theory.   2. Postmodernism—Social aspects.
3. Motherhood—United States—History—19th century.
I. Title.
HQ1190.C48   1995
306.874'3'097309034—dc20   94–13186

1 2 3 4 5 00 99 98 97 96 95

CONTENTS

Preface vii

Acknowledgments xv

1. The Limits of Liberal Discourse 1
   Non/White Women of the Republic

2. Charlotte Temple's Remains 24

3. Revivification and Utopian Time 41
   Poe versus Stowe

4. "Strange Coincidence" 61
   Disavowal and History in Hawthorne and Cummins

5. "Your Mother Is Here" 92
   Harriet Jacobs and the Decommodification of Motherhood

 Postscript 112
   Postmodern Subjectivity and Virtual Motherhood

Notes 133

Works Cited 148

Index 154

for Lucy Cherniavsky
(Anyukámnak)

Preface

He tried to drink, and revel, and swear away the
memory; but often, in the deep night, whose solemn
stillness arraigns the bad soul in forced communion
with herself, he had seen that pale mother rising by
his bedside, and felt the soft twining of that hair
around his fingers, till the cold sweat would run down
his face, and he would spring from his bed in horror.
　　　—Harriet Beecher Stowe, *Uncle Tom's Cabin*

I'll be your lover from the womb to the tomb
I'll dress as your daughter when the moon becomes round
You'll be my mother when everything's gone.
　　　—The Pretenders, "Hymn to Her"

As the effects of a subtle and politically enforced
performativity, gender is an "act," as it were, that is
open to splittings, self-parody, self-criticism, and
those hyperbolic exhibitions of "the natural" that, in
their very exaggeration, reveal its fundamentally
phantasmatic status.
　　　—Judith Butler, *Gender Trouble*

This project is concerned with questions raised by the vexed status of motherhood in current Euro-American feminist critical theory. If postmodernism signifies the end of origin stories, is motherhood a residually modern phenomenon? Do we (should we) imagine, with Julia Kristeva, that the mother is the "strange fold that changes culture into nature, the speaking into biology," a being who exists—and endures—beyond her historical determinations, to the eternal embarrassment of anti-foundationalist feminisms? How do we (con)figure a non-original motherhood? The directions of Euro-American feminist critical work in the past twenty years might suggest that motherhood is hopelessly mired in reproductive nature, and its politics inextricably linked to the bourgeois family, even though the second of these propositions would appear to undermine the first, by referring us to the historical specificity of what counts as "natural," to the non-originality of nature (or reproduction). From this vantage, the problem of motherhood for postmodern feminisms derives not from the essentially ahistorical quality of women's reproductive lives but from the continuing ability of a bourgeois discourse on motherhood to render its assumptions transparent.

When in the early to mid-1980s feminist women of color began to intervene in the so-called mainstream of Euro-American feminism, they aimed to expose and critique the bourgeois ideologies of gendered, individual, and collective identity that continued to inform both mainstream critical discourse and political action. Euro-American feminists were compelled, or in Donna Haraway's phrase, "were forced kicking and screaming" to recognize how race, class, ethnicity, and sexuality informed their identity as women and its historical privileges. But the consequence was less a rescripting than a nervous evasion of the bourgeois maternal body that had been, up until that point, central to Anglo-American and French feminisms alike. There were, of course, those who simply continued to talk of object relations or *écriture feminine,* as though little had occurred to displace the centrality of such analytical concepts to feminist critical work. Progressive white feminists turned instead to the modelling of contingent (hybrid-ized; ironized) female bodies; thus to such influential models as Audre Lorde's biomythography of lesbian community or Gloria Anzaldúa's *mestiza* we can add by the mid to late 1980s Donna Haraway's cyborg or Judith Butler's model of performative gender.

My purpose is not to upbraid Haraway, Butler or any other progressive feminist for failing to think critically about motherhood (as though any particular critic had an obligation to do so) but simply to remark that the bourgeois maternal body has been left curiously intact in/by current academic feminist critical discourses. Meanwhile, from *Blade Runner* to *thirtysomething* to the contemporary debates on abortion and surrogacy, naturalized motherhood pervades late-twentieth-century U.S. culture, exerting a dominance that demands—continues to demand—a reckoning. If as Frederic Jameson argues, postmodernism is the cultural dominant of this late capitalist moment, a modern foundationalist discourse of motherhood persists amid the radical alteration of the cultural and historical conditions of its production.[1] It seems we can still somehow believe, with Margaret Fuller, that "man is of woman born, and her face bends over him in infancy with an expression he can never quite forget." Under these conditions, we need a feminist history that seeks to deauthenticate rather than (re)mythologize Fuller's conception of motherhood. *That Pale Mother Rising* aims to model this kind of a revisionist approach to motherhood. I align Fuller's understanding of the maternal body, as the lost origin and the affective trace of man's essential identity, with democratic political formation and bourgeois sociality; and I argue that as a politically enforced act, essential motherhood resolves into a more or less parodic and oppositional imitation.

Feminist "history" in this sense implies something other than a (re)construction of the past as the context of and complement to the present. Such a "history" necessarily distances itself from what is still (arguably) the dominant historiographical mode, in which it is the function of the historian to mark origins, track development, and attain a density of reference suggestive of coverage. To

produce this kind of foundationalist historical knowledge under
the aegis of a specifically postmodern critical practice would be at
the very least incongruous. Rather, this project draws on what
Walter Benjamin famously defines as the materialist critique of
history (a model I engage more fully in chapter 4), in which the
writing of history requires an engagement with the past that
disrupts the coherence or integrity of the present tense. For
Benjamin, the point is to "blast open" history's "continuum," or in
other words—eliding for the moment Benjamin's loaded
metaphor—to apprehend the alterity of history, and (as) the
possibility of alternative futures. My investment here is not to map
the genesis and proliferation of the discourse of essential motherhood, nor to demonstrate its continuity in early national culture.
Beginning more or less where the foundationalist historical project
leaves off, with the claim that the discourse of essential motherhood is a representative feature of the early national period (from
roughly the 1780s to the Civil War), I aim instead to defamiliarize and disarticulate this discursive formation. From this vantage,
the postscript on "Postmodern Subjectivity and Virtual Motherhood" is not incidental to my reading of nineteenth-century
sentimentalism but crucially locates my historical investment in
the present—in the writing of a history which enables different
continuations.

The disarticulation of essential motherhood hinges on a double
claim. First, as I have already suggested, that essential motherhood,
as codified in the discourse of sentimentalism, is remarkably stylized: exaggerated; overwrought; improvised; seamed. Second, that
essential motherhood is the dominant but not the only register for
the representation of the reproductive body in this period. Essential motherhood needs to be read with and against the juridical
determination of the African-American mother, for whom motherhood reduces to an ambiguously signifying "condition" (i.e., the
child follows the condition of the mother). Drawing on African-
American feminist work, and especially on Hortense Spillers's
understanding of the African-American mother as a particular

modality of gendered existence in an "American grammar," I argue that the existence of the "conditional" African-American mother on the discursive margins of white middle-class culture tends to expose the equally contingent status of a supposedly original white motherhood. A revisionist approach to original motherhood thus begins by apprehending whiteness as a racial identity rather than as the absence of racial encoding. Because the reproductive body of the African-American is historically not comprehended in/ by the discourse of original motherhood, her representation in the sentimental text racializes reproductive nature. *Both* the commodified (black) *and* the naturalized (white) reproductive bodies become at least potentially legible in their contingency, as bodies articulated in opposition to each other (i.e., mothers are not black; black women are not mothers).[2]

The first two chapters align essentialized motherhood with Enlightenment concepts of identity and democratic principles of representation. While other versions of essential motherhood clearly predate the Enlightenment, I argue that what we are left to unravel today is a specifically modern paradigm, in which the mother grounds or guarantees a rational political order by being made to embody the politically impure, the nonrational political alliances and affinities that "consensual" democracy proscribes. The bourgeois mother marks the boundary, not between nature and culture, or between excess in general and the law as such, but between proscribed and legitimate forms of political behavior in a specific historical context. The first chapter further considers how this notion of the mother as limit finds its own limit in the figure of the commodified reproductive body, in a doubling and disarticulation of a dominant logic graphically rendered in Thomas Jefferson's representation of black albino slaves. Chapter 2 reads the early American seduction novel, as exemplified by Susanna Rowson's *Charlotte Temple* and Hannah Foster's *The Coquette,* as a genre which understands liminal motherhood to be a specifically political, rather than an original determination of the maternal body, and hence open to strategies of political subversion.

Chapter 3 pursues this analysis in a discussion of antebellum sentimental discourse, pairing Edgar Allan Poe's "Ligeia" with Harriet Beecher Stowe's *Uncle Tom's Cabin.* Both these texts may be read as interrogating the mother's expulsion from history and the political. However, the narrator of "Ligeia" can only recapitulate the mother's exclusion as the condition of his own intelligibility; in contrast, Stowe's slave mother Cassy impersonates the figure of the essential white mother in a gesture that reconfigures corporeal essence as style. Cassy's presence in the text suggests how the commodified black female body inhabits the discourse of sentimentalism, as a counterpossibility to the political proscriptions that the original (white) maternal body serves to naturalize (legitimate).

The following three chapters each develop the discussion of Poe and Stowe along a different critical axis. Chapter 4, which reads Nathaniel Hawthorne's *The Blithedale Romance* with and against Maria Susanna Cummins's *The Lamplighter,* also pairs a masculinist with a proto-feminist sentimental text. But in its focus on fetishism, and particularly on the fetishist's relation to history and discursive authority, this chapter is conceptually aligned with the section on Poe. Conversely, chapter 5 extends the discussion of performative motherhood to Harriet Jacobs's *Incidents in the Life of a Slave Girl,* understood as a subaltern rewriting of Stowe's sentimental paradigm. I argue that Jacobs both legitimates her claim to her children on the basis of natural maternal affection and deftly denaturalizes bourgeois motherhood, which is refigured in her text as a politically resonant affectation.

The postscript extends the discussion of fetishism to postmodern culture, through a reading of contemporary reproductive discourse (on surrogacy, *in vitro* fertilization, the "cybernetic womb") and of William Gibson's cult novel *Neuromancer.* Technologically mediated motherhood is not necessarily denaturalized; in fact, the virtual womb functions in *Neuromancer* as the perfected fetish object, in which the denizens of cyberspace disavow the loss of an original maternal plenitude. However, my reading of Gibson's novel also tracks an alternative in the figure of the cyborg Molly, who suggests how the interface of the organic and the cybernetic might be successfully claimed as the site of a transformative reproductive politics. Drawing on Donna Haraway's notion, that her cyborg is a "polychromatic girl . . . a girl who's not trying to become Woman, but remain responsible to women of many colors and positions," I decipher in Molly's improvised techno-body the terms of a discourse of polychromatic motherhood.

The first version of this project, begun about six years ago, addressed the writing of the maternal body in antebellum American culture from the vantage of French feminist theory, primarily the work of Julia Kristeva and Luce Irigaray. Before the first draft was complete, the focus had already begun to shift, from a study of the maternal body as an excess disruptive of cultural codes, to an examination of how the excessive maternal body functioned *as* a regulative cultural code. But in an important sense, this project inhabits at its origin the historical formation it seeks to unravel. If, as I argue here, the maternal marks the site (the "fold") in modern democratic order where the political is transformed into the affective, then the difficulty from the vantage of a late-twentieth-century, radical democratic feminism is to rethink the maternal as both a political *and* an affective structure. Since beginning this book, I have come to a markedly different political understanding of the sentimental codes mobilized in The Pretenders "Hymn to Her," and across the spectrum of both popular and elite feminist cultures in the U.S. I am still learning how to be, if not indifferent to the appeal these lyrics rehearse, at least differently moved by them.

Acknowledgments

It is a pleasure to acknowledge the many people who read and responded generously and with much critical intelligence to various portions and drafts of this project: Kathleen Biddick, Patrick Brantlinger, Mitchell Breitwieser (under whose direction this project was initiated), Helen Deutsch, Jonathan Elmer, Thomas Foster, Susan Gubar, Katherine Hayles, Susan Jeffords, Christoph Lohmann, Terence Martin, Carolyn Mitchell, Carolyn Porter, Stephen Rachman, Sean Rosenheim, Mary Ryan, and Stephanie Smith. I am indebted to the members of two graduate seminars I offered in the Spring of 1991 and 1993, especially Kari Bloedel, Wes Cecil, Susan Clements, Carol Guess, Elizabeth Kuhlmann, Ashley Tidey, and Yung-Hsing Wu, whose conversation on issues closely related to this project contributed significantly to its final form. To Helen Deutsch, Kate McCullough, and, especially, Thomas Foster, I owe an inextricably personal and professional debt, both for keeping reality on line and distracting me from it.

The postscript to this study originally appeared in *Genders* 18 (Winter 1993) and is reprinted here by the generous permission of the University of Texas Press. My thanks to Joan Catapano, Senior Sponsoring Editor at Indiana University Press. I am grateful as well to Indiana University for a Summer Faculty Fellowship in 1992 and to the Department of English for a semester of supported leave.

THAT
PALE
MOTHER
RISING

1 The Limits of Liberal Discourse

Non/White Women of the Republic

> Some man would learn a good deal
> about her in the talk, never altogether
> truly, for Melanctha all her life did not
> know how to tell a story wholly.
> She always, and yet not with intention,
> managed to leave out big pieces which
> make a story very different, for when
> it came to what had happened and
> what she had said and what it was she
> had really done, Melanctha never
> could remember right.
> —Gertrude Stein

My title invokes Linda Kerber's groundbreaking history *Women of the Republic* in order at once to recall and defamiliarize its categories—to remember this history differently.[1] I want to interrogate further the gendering of republican womanhood by resisting the self-evidence of "women" as a category of historical analysis, to ask instead who counts as a woman in this rationalized social and political order, a question which in more ways than one requires a calculus of absent and elided bodies. First, because middle-class white women are precisely un(ac)counted (for) in the republican symbolic, they represent the unquantifiable, the in-excess of the representative social body.[2] For Kerber, notwithstanding republican women's legal invisibility and lack of political representation, the duties of the republican woman, particularly her status as inculcator of civic virtue in her children, constitute a specific form of participation in the *polis*. While I would agree that this idealization of motherhood is central to the constitution of liberal democracy,[3] I argue that the idealized mother in no sense materializes as a political subject; rather, the white middle-class mother is positioned at/as the phantasmatic limit of the political order. Second, we need to think the disappearances that inform the category "women" inasmuch as not all sexed female bodies are gendered feminine. To read the republican construction of womanhood as unquantifiable is to read the concept of "women" with and against the legal and economic determinations of the black woman's body, who finds herself the object of the most relentless quantification, against a body that reduces to an enumeration of commodified functions, that becomes, in Hortense Spillers's dense and suggestive formulation, "ungendered."[4] Thus a double disappearance organizes the discourse of republican womanhood: the exclusion of "women" from the abstract social body, and the exclusion of marked female bodies from the category "women."

Here my project is to examine this placement of "women" at the constitutive limit of the political, and of the racialized body at the constitutive limit of the category "women," in the foundational discourses of the political order's designers.[5] Although in the context of white women's disenfranchisement and of black women's social death, few of the founders' texts have much to say about the status of either white or black women as such, I will argue that these texts delineate and deploy gendered categories of knowledge and representation. Moreover, this chapter is particularly concerned with the disposition of white and black women's bodies in Thomas Jefferson's *Notes on the State of Virginia,* as a text which quite explicitly addresses women's place in a naturalized social order. The *Notes* simultaneously naturalize women's liminal relation to the legitimate modalities of political agency as the apparent consequence, or cultural articulation, of the woman's sex, and invoke race as a category which functions precisely to interrupt the mirror play of the sex/gender couple. In this sense, my reading of the *Notes* invites an understanding of republican womanhood significantly different from Kerber's. Rather than a discourse on gender which simply fails to extend to the black woman in slavery, so that gender remains thinkable without reference to race (as Kerber's study tends to imply), republican womanhood stands as a discourse on femininity which operates only on *condition* of the black woman's exclusion. This revision of republican womanhood demands a shift of critical emphasis, so that we interrogate not only how slavery denies black women a womanhood to which black women naturally have title, but also how the discursive naturalization of womanhood serves the interests of white supremacist patriarchy. As Judith Butler points out, we need to consider gender not merely as the cultural interpretation of given, or biological sex, but as "the discursive/cultural means by which 'sexed nature' or 'a natural sex' is produced and established as 'prediscursive,' prior to culture, a politically neutral surface on which culture acts."[6] To treat the black woman's exclusion from the collective body of "womanhood" as a kind of lapse in the recognition of her natural, or given, sexual identity, is to miss the import of the way that the condition of the black woman in slavery throws the contingency of naturalized gender into political relief.[7]

If, as Hortense Spillers contends, we can speak of gender only in relation to a gendered *subject,* so that given the radical objectification of the black man and woman in slavery, the destruction of the familial/domestic, the "theft of the body itself . . . we lose at least gender difference in the outcome,"[8] it is worth considering that white supremacist discourse assigns a "sexed nature" to the "ungendered" body precisely so as to naturalize this *loss.* For instance, by inscribing the black woman as a "breeder," white supremacist discourse produces the body on which motherhood naturally reduces to the reproduction of property. While on the white woman's body the inscription of her "sexed nature" naturalizes a particular gender performance, on the black woman's body her "sexed nature" functions conversely to legitimate her "ungendering." With respect to the black woman's "nature" as a commodity, feminine gender thus becomes a thing to claim, assume, or strategically to affect. In this frame, I will argue that the anxiety which disorders Jefferson's text develops from the difficulty not only of refusing to the black woman the "natural" privileges of her sex, but of confining to the black woman's body alone the spectacle of a merely contingent femininity. For Jefferson, this amounts to preventing its migration by keeping the black woman's body out of the cultural discourse. Finding her way nonetheless into Jefferson's text, in the complexly liminal form of a black "albino," a non/white woman on the boundary of "her" own (un)making, she claims a place in my text as the first in a series of women whose boundary crossings call into question what and where "women" are said to be.

I advance this reading of the *Notes* as part of a larger contention, then, crucial to this book as a whole, that the understanding of femininity/motherhood as limit, variously and richly engaged in a number of contemporary critical registers,[9] can only be politically adequate if pursued in tandem with an interrogation into the limits of femininity/motherhood—into motherhood as a historical discourse. A (re)valorization of motherhood as essentially liminal to symbolic order in no way displaces what this limit centers. The mother's liminality, her location at/as the origin, or pre-text, of the individuated (acculturated) subject, needs to be thought historically, as contingent on the emergence of a specifically modern subjectivity, constituted in democratic representation and bourgeois sociality. Furthermore, in order to think liminal motherhood historically, we need also to (re)think this dehistoricization of the white maternal body (as what is prior to acculturation) in relation to the commodification of the African-American reproductive body. Thus my aim is emphatically *not* to suggest an analogy on the model of "just as white women are debarred from the political, black women are debarred from white womanhood"—an analogy which precisely reproduces a hierarchy of racial and sexual difference. On the contrary, I wish to explore the political and affective *nonequivalence* between white women's displacement from the social as origin, and black women's displacement from liminal womanhood as commodity, and its consequence: that the black female body assumes its ironic critical privilege as the site where the contingency of generic/gender designations suddenly passes into view.

To interrogate the placement of raced and sexed bodies in Jefferson's text is to address their constitution in, and in opposition to, the bourgeois epistemology Stein derides in the epigraph to this chapter, to the desire for a "wholly" rationalized subject that reduces bodies to abstraction and renders inarticulable the heterogeneous remainder. But I begin with Stein as much for her reproduction of such a rationalist reduction as for her satiric reduction of the reductionist: Melanctha's deficiency, her inability to "remember right," is no less the object of the narrator's amusement in this passage than "some man['s]" aspiration to complete knowledge of her. If the point is that this black woman's multiple and contradictory standpoints render her only partially and differently knowable, why does Melanctha here assume the burden of the white man's rationalism as the mark of her own inadequacy?[10] Stein's disclosure of "women's" difference at the site of the African-American female body in this text resists the patriarchal reduction of (white) feminine alterity, even as it replicates such a reduction with respect to the black woman's difference; the sign of race in "Melanctha" is the lack of "intention," of verbal competence, Melanctha's incapacity to know what she means.[11] This overemphatic characterization of Melanctha's lapses suggest that the narrator here disavows what she knows to be the "truth" of Melanctha's accounting. We might caption the narrator's portrait of Melanctha this way: "I know the partial story is the only adequate one, but all the same I will make it Melanctha's inadequacy."[12] In this sense, Stein achieves what Jefferson does *not:* a strategy of sustained ambivalence. Jefferson's black albino women place rationalist epistemology in crisis, and exact his queasy acknowledgment of a "very different" rendering.

Speaking Wholly: The Politics of Closure

It is certainly not a novel observation that the bourgeois rationalization of social and political relations comprehended under the term "liberalism" transpires differently in Europe than in the United States, where the discourses of liberal democracy more effectively reduce the modalities of oppositional politics and restrict the range of intelligible dissent.[13] In what has become the traditional account of this disparity, the consolidation of the political field in the United States is ascribed to America's elision of history, to the absence of the pre-existing class antagonisms that characterized contemporary European societies, an absence which constitutes, so this polemic goes, the decisive circumstance of the nation's founding. Thus Myra Jehlen, in *American Incarnation* (1986):

> In Europe, when Natural Law theorists such as Locke and Rousseau contended that the natural sanctity of the individual and the equally natural equipoise of the market dictated a democratic system of government based on contracts and laws, they were inevitably conscious, even as they appealed to nature, of the historical context of preexisting alternative forms [. . .] [In contrast] America was an avatar of the world prior to feudalism. . . . Responding only to nature (as it had no history), American civilization remained at one with it and embodied nature's laws organically, as the adult embodies the child rather than as a painting represents the landscape. . . . And in the reconciled natural civilization that once and for all transcended the old world's successive dialectical compromises, [the European immigrant] assumed a natural, therefore absolute and not politically disputable dominion.[14]

In one possible reading of this comparative analysis—if we read it as a critical analysis—Jehlen calls for a dismantling of "America," as this dangerously compelling phantasm of a space outside of history, in which the ideological categories of Enlightenment political theory pretend to transcend their historical determinations. Elsewhere, however, Jehlen's tersely rendered premise forecloses on this interpretation of her argument; as the historical blank slate on which to inscribe the "absolute dominion" of the Western self, "America" assumes for her the status of an objectively given space: "[T]he decisive factor shaping the founding conceptions of 'America' and 'the American' was material *rather than* conceptual; rather than a set of abstract ideas, the physical fact of the continent."[15] From this perspective, the material would stand in opposition to the conceptual in the mode of given "fact" to "abstraction," as though the determination of the factual was not precisely a labor of conceptualization, a function of historically situated categories of knowledge. As dehistoricized matter is here made to originate the concept of "America," the Western self falls in love with its image all over again—a narrative which in this retelling no longer serves to legitimate the subjugation and genocide of non-Western peoples, but only because it seems to posit them as always already deleted. At the very least, Jehlen's literalizing construction of such a "reconciled natural civilization" expunges the Native American, whose presence fractures the myth of "America's" pre-symbolic integrity; and the African, whose forced labor betrays the all too plainly interested construction of American nature as exploitable resource, as the soil of capitalist expansion.[16]

What strikes me in Jehlen's argument as the highly problematic remystification of "America" in one sense at least points less to a critical failure of imagination on Jehlen's part than to her success; the difficulty here lies with the very concept of an American Incarnation, which Jehlen inherits from the "Exceptionalist" critical tradition and elaborates only too eloquently. Such a concept serves to occlude both the violence to the material world of the white man's conceptualization of it (where the "material" is understood as neither abstraction, nor "physical fact," but as the historically contingent conditions of existence of human and non-human life), and the presence of multiple forces of actual and potential resistance that make "America" at its *origins* a *contested zone*. The apparent capacity of American liberal democracy to consume heterogeneous futures so that, in Jefferson's formulation, if any transgress the law, "their acts shall become nullities"[17] neither requires nor even implies the absence of historically determined resistance.[18] The very excessiveness of liberal order as Jefferson represents it, where transgression annuls itself in its encounter with the law and the ground of radical political contestation recedes, eternally, to the horizon,[19] suggests instead that the specific historical conditions of America's colonization engender an all too disturbing set of insurrectionary possibilities, which results in a particularly violent policing of political borders. From this perspective it may appear that the American political order conceives itself not on the compliant body of American nature but on particularly divided terrain.

Marxist critique has often and productively explained the evacuation of contingent material, or "content," which in Jehlen's argument represents the *condition* of the political order's foundation, as an *effect* of a closed, or totalizing, rationalism. As Georg Lukács notes, "it is clear what the problem of the actually given means for rationalism: viz. that it cannot be left to its own being and existence, for in that case it would remain ineluctably 'contingent.' Instead it must be wholly absorbed into the rational system of the concepts of the understanding."[20] Ironically, Jehlen would no doubt embrace Lukács's analysis (elsewhere she does so explicitly); she ostensibly respects (in fact privileges) the (f)actual as that which exceeds its determination by the bourgeois "concept." However, in Jehlen's construction, we find the (f)actual precisely divested of its historical contingency, so as not to contradict but to solicit its own reduction under the rationalist's inclusive gaze. Thus the "actually given" appears to hand us ready-made the very thing that it by definition overflows—the abstract categories of "Natural Law."

Yet the crucial Marxist insight into the operations of bourgeois rationalism lies in attributing rationalism's omnivorousness, its trademark negation of its own partiality, not to a disposition on the part of the material consumed, but to the irrationality of rational system itself. As Theodor Adorno observes, a rational order posited as universal must also, impossibly, encompass its own exterior:

Out of itself, the bourgeois *ratio* undertook to produce the order it had negated outside itself. Once produced, however, that order ceased to be an order and was therefore insatiable. Every system was such an order, such an absurdly rational product; a posited thing posing as being-in-itself. Its origins had to be placed into formal thought divorced from content; nothing else would let it control the material.[21]

In order to posit a contingent thing as "being-in-itself," to effect the system's colonization of what is definitionally outside its borders, the Founding Fathers must derive it whole, *as* a system, or logic of representation, abstracted from what it systematizes/represents—in a gesture Jacques Derrida aligns *not* with America's ahistoricity but with the temporality of the written declaration, of a textual founding.[22] In other words, the rational totalization of the political field depends on a system of representation conceptually autonomous from the particular subjects whose political representation it supposedly assures. The particularized, or embodied, subject remains as such unrepresentable; the subject's specificity is precisely what is voided in his accession to the status of citizen.[23]

As *The Federalist* insists, the constitution which recognizes the rights and obligations of citizenship has a minimal positive content. Rather than a compendium of laws for the determination of particular individual and institutional prerogatives and restraints, the force of which would reside in its exhaustive consideration of specific eventualities, the Constitution furnishes principles designed exactly to *prevent the incursion of the particular,* to render all possible contestatory actions decipherable within the classifications of liberal order itself (even, indeed especially, those oppositional acts of which the founders cannot conceive), and thus reducible in and to the logic of the very system whose legitimacy would be in contention. In James Madison's elaboration, constitutionally vested power functions to uphold itself, as the limit of the representable.[24]

Had the convention attempted a positive enumeration of the powers necessary and proper for carrying their [the governing bodies] other

> powers into effect, the attempt would have involved a complete digest
> of laws on every subject to which the Constitution relates; accommo-
> dated too not only to the existing state of things, but *to all the possible
> changes which futurity may produce.*
> [. . .] Had they attempted to enumerate the particular powers or means
> not necessary or proper for carrying the general powers into execution,
> the task would have been no less chimerical; and would have been liable
> to this further objection, that every defect in the enumeration would
> have been equivalent to a positive grant of authority.
> [. . .] *No axiom is more clearly established in law, or in reason, than that
> wherever the end is required, the means are authorized;* wherever a general
> power to do a thing is given, every particular power necessary for doing
> it is included.[25]

An enumeration, or digest, of political powers would inevitably
particularize the institutional bodies it defines and thus produce a
merely partial legal and political formation. In the attempt to
specify the innumerable transgressions of the law with which the
law is *a priori* commensurate, the founders would produce a more
or less incomplete catalogue that only misconstrues the object it
describes. Rather than specify the law's domain, in a gesture which
necessarily circumscribes it, the founders frame the law as the rational determination of the unspecifiable. The law polices the limit
of the representable by abstracting the unrepresentable as a category of legal knowledge, to become Adorno's "absurdly rational
product," a system that appropriates its own beyond. From "out of
itself," rational system "produces" its excess as its concept, as the
infinitely capacious body of "all the possible changes which futu-
rity may produce," and on which liberal order conceives its transhistorical identity.

Liminal Womanhood and Diffusive Sympathy

If material life in its contingency crosses and exceeds rational
categories of distinction, rational order produces the material

(from "out of itself") as an unspecifiable whole. Madison's delineation of legitimate political acts reduces particular oppositional actions and eventualities to the unrepresentable totality of "all . . . possible" oppositional acts, in and against which the law derives itself as a universal discourse. Here I want to consider how the critique of American political order makes visible the relation between a specifically political category of unrepresentable prospects and the white female body. The project is to think the relation between femininity and the unrepresentable historically *not* as a function of women's relation to *the* symbolic but as a function of their relation to historically specific symbolic organizations; to one marked, in this instance, by the disavowal of its own partiality, by the elevation of fetishism to the status of a cultural logic. In this section, I situate in the discourse of sympathy a historically specific convergence of femininity and the unrepresentable to suggest that democratic culture domesticates the infinitely large and formless figure of "all . . . possible" nonrational forms and affinities in the body of the white middle-class mother.

Of course, the maternal body as such does not figure in the founders' explicitly political discourse, which addresses the rights and obligations of (white male) citizenship under the law.[26] But if it is not possible to produce evidence for this politicized understanding of motherhood *in* the founders' texts, it is possible to trace an analogy between the configuration of the nonrational in Madison's scripting of the political and the configuration of the maternal body in the bourgeois scripting of the subject. The connection finds support in Madison's use of the term "sympathy," a term encoded in contemporary American seduction novels as a specifically *feminine/maternal* medium.

> On the same principle, the more multitudinous a representative assembly may be rendered, the more it will partake of the infirmities incident to collective meetings of the people. Ignorance will be the dupe of cunning, and passion the slave of sophistry and declamation. The people can never err more than in supposing that by multiplying their representatives

> beyond a certain limit they strengthen the barrier against the government
> of a few. Experience will forever admonish them that, on the contrary,
> *after securing a sufficient number for the purposes of safety, of local infor-*
> *mation, and of diffusive sympathy with the whole society,* they will counteract
> their own views by every addition to their representatives. The counte-
> nance of the government may become more democratic, but the soul that
> animates it will be more oligarchic.[27]

A representative body that too exactly coincides with the accumu-
lated bodies of the people represented curiously loses its status as
a democratic representation of "the people"—loses its connection
to "the whole society." The constitutive logic of this social whole
should be familiar: as a rational entity, "the whole society" must
encompass the unrepresentable materiality of the social body.
Significantly, however, the representative here "produces" the
unrepresentable (from "out of itself") in the form of affect, or "sympathy"; "the people" as a material community are absorbed into
the democratic social whole as a sensation of connection engendered in the abstract body of "the representative assembly." In this
context, we need to (re)think the identification of reproductive
femininity with sympathy in the early national cultural imaginary.
Most prominently, it is the sentimental discourse of the novel
which thematizes and mobilizes this notion of sympathetic
motherhood. But my point is that the sentimental representation
of motherhood needs to be sited as articulating a logic endemic to
the period of national founding; *and* as codifying an understanding of the reproductive (white) female body widely central to
the representation of bourgeois subjectivity, up to and including
psychoanalysis.[28]

That is, I want to insist on the specifically nationalist resonance
of the term "sympathy": while women are excluded from political
representation, the maternal body acquires an essentially social
affect.[29] To say this is to assert both more and less than does Linda
Kerber on the measure of women's inclusion in the *polis*. Whereas
Kerber reads women's disenfranchisement as a regrettable incon-
sistency, as the founders' betrayal of the democratic principles they

espouse, I read the exclusion of women from political representation, and their legal incapacity to form contractual relations, as an *index to* the logic of American foundationalist discourse: insofar as white women's social presence reduces to the purely affective, early national culture successfully produces the white female body from "out of itself" as the sensationalized trace of a rationalized materiality. Likewise, in Kerber's view, the social idealization of the mother-child bond enables women's civic participation in a domestic register. But if disenfranchised republican women are not simply or effectually ejected from public life, white women's accession to a socially affective corporeality leaves at best uncertain their relation to political agency.

I want to insist, as well, on the centrality of sympathetic, or affective, motherhood to the structure of bourgeois identity—to insist that reproductive femininity *is* consistently reduced to affective corporeality in bourgeois discourses on the subject. Such a reduction informs, for example, Freud's famous articulation of (masculine) subjectivity in the fort/da game, as forged in ironic mastery over the mother's loss. Freud's construction of maternal presence as what is originally lost to the individuated subject equates her presence with *full* presence, and so (dis)places the mother-child relation into the register of the phantasmatic: by identifying the mother with the possibility of integral being, Freud (re)situates her as an affecting absence, as a yearning for death/completion, in the individuated subject. The mother thus assumes the same position in Freud's narrative of the subject as does the whole society in Madison's narrative of the democratic nation, with the difference that Freud recognizes, as Madison does not, the incommensurability of differentiation (or life) and closure. Moreover, Freud's understanding of maternal presence as what is originally lost finds its popular echo in the sentimental *bildungsroman,* and the genre's thematic of the motherless (orphaned) child.

The connection I am sketching here, between a certain conception of affective motherhood on the one hand (one which turns decisively on the mother's absence from the domain of subjectivity, her status as anterior to the social symbolic), and a logic of democratic representation on the other, finds interesting confirmation in Philippe Lacoue-Labarthe's and Jean-Luc Nancy's co-authored essays on the closure of the political field in contemporary liberal democracies. The main concern of these essays is with the corollary, or effect, of such closure which the authors describe as "le retrait du politique," the withdrawal "of the political itself, as a specific dimension, or as the dimension of a specific alterity."[30] Lacoue-Labarthe and Nancy discern a double exigency in the face of this withdrawal. In Nancy Fraser's summary of their argument, "the closure of the political . . . requires us to think the *re-trait* in two senses: first, as a *withdrawal* on our part from the blinding self-evidence of the political, which marks our confinement in its closure; and second, as a *retracing* of the political from the standpoint of its essence."[31] This essence—or "specific alterity"—of the political assumes for Lacoue-Labarthe and Nancy a variety of different guises (among other things, the essence of the political is "philosophy"—hence their call to specifically "philosophical research" on political order).[32] But in at least two of its determinations, the essence of the political converges with what I have called the unrepresentable in/of the democratic symbolic. First, the alterity of the political consists for Lacoue-Labarthe and Nancy in "a relation of the community to itself where it can present or represent for itself its common being as such."[33] In this sense, the essence of the political is "the unity, the totality, and . . . the effective manifestation of the community," a communal "totality" which (I have argued) finds its purely affective manifestation in Madison's conception of a representative body.[34] Second, their discussion of community and "the social bond" [le lien social] brings them home, via the question of the subject, to the place of the mother:

> We will content ourselves today with underscoring this: if the "social bond" constitutes a veritable question—and, by the same token, consti-

tutes a limit-question—for Freud, it is insofar as the given [social] relation (we want to say: the relation such as, after all, Freud gives it to himself, such as he *presupposes* it, he too, like all of philosophy), the relation
between a subject and subjectivity itself in the figure of the father, implies, at the origin or in the guise of an origin, the birth (or, precisely, the
gift) of this relation. And such a birth implies the withdrawal of what is
neither subject, nor object, nor figure, and that one can, provisionally or
in the interest of simplicity, call "the mother." Behind the political (if one
must identify it with the Father), stands "the mother."[35]

Here the "effective manifestation" of the social bond, that is to say,
of the community's relation to itself, is withdrawn into the formless non-figure of the mother, who incorporates the essential alterity of the subject with respect to the political order.[36]

I am interested in this formulation for its peculiar capitulation
to the logic of a closure that it is precisely the writers' project to
query. While acknowledging the political character of what is
withdrawn from the totalized political field, they elect to engage
this material *as* essence, to valorize its exteriority to the domain of
liberal democratic politics: the alterity of the political thus remains
extrinsic to the scene of its production—extrinsic to the discursive
order that produces it as other. But inasmuch as the mother's essential exteriority to the zone of subjectivity is a function of a
specific logic of representation, to retrace the subject from the
standpoint of this maternal body is to rediscover the subject of
liberal democratic discourse, rather than to contest the determinations of the subject within a totalized political system. Instead,
I would suggest that our withdrawal from the "blinding self-
evidence" of the political and/or of "the subject" requires our critique of the mother's position as essence. The problematic of
essential or originary motherhood emerges in the author's telling
choice of the locution "behind" to designate the mother's place.
This locution draws incongruously on the famous freudian ar-
chaeological model (and its equation of the maternal with the
Minoan). But the possibility, implicit in the term "behind," of dis-
interring and recuperating something prior to representation is ex-

actly what Lacoue-Labarthe and Nancy reject. On the contrary, they emphasize that what has been withdrawn "perhaps in fact never took place,"[37] and that (consequently) there can be no question of simply exiting the political from its withdrawal (restoring us to a logic of full presence), only of engaging its alterity in a manner that refuses any (new) foundationalist project.[38] As Nancy Fraser observes, the authors themselves strangely withdraw from what such a project seems to entail—the engagement of this alterity at the level of contingent political relations: "When they problematize the contemporary truism that 'everything is political' and suggest instead that 'behind the political (if it must be identified with the Father), lies the mother,' Nancy and Lacoue-Labarthe at once gesture at and recoil from questions now being posed by Western feminists . . . [The current wave of feminist scholarship] remains engaged while problematizing extant concepts and institutions of the political and avoids the snares of transcendentalism by incorporating empirical and normative elements into its philosophical critique."[39] The feminist scholarship on which Lacoue-Labarthe and Nancy might productively draw, in other words, resists the lure of the transcendent to produce the maternal and/or the alterity of the political not as essence but as the possibility of a transformative politics.

"Women" on the Verge

In other words, Lacoue-Labarthe and Nancy fail to engage the mother as the "non-figure" of a political alterity produced from "out of" liberal democracy—whose essentialization as the difference of this closed political order from itself only supports the logic of closure. More usefully, we can engage the closure of the political field, and the mother's relation to subjectivity, by locating her "non-figure" with respect to other (con)figurations of motherhood. Jefferson's representation of black albino women sites the limit of essentialized motherhood on the commodified body of the female slave. On the bodies of these women, who fall outside the discourse of the gender that they wear (in the form of whiteness), the coherence of feminine gender is compromised and the discursive space of motherhood decolonized, reclaimed as a locus of contestatory representations.

These women make their appearance in the *Notes* as mute figures, a designated "anomaly of nature," wedged between an entry on native birds and remarks on the importation of the honey bee. They are as such less the agents of resistance than an emblem of Jefferson's dis-ease. But despite their status in the *Notes* as silenced and objectified figures, I would argue that they display an irreducible material remainder of the rationalized black body.[40] The women's resistance to the rationalist's consuming gaze is encoded in the "perpetual tremulous vibration" of their eyes: they neither submit to Jefferson's gaze (as objects), nor seek to return it on its own terms (as the subjects in and of rational discourse). Instead they suspend the dialectic, refusing both subjection and rational subjectivity, maintaining a flickering presence in the text that permanently eludes the logic of Jefferson's representation. From this perspective, their appearance in the *Notes* (published in 1787, the same year as publication of the *The Federalist* commenced)[41] places resisting bodies at the scene of the nation's founding and thus serves to remind us that the erection of democratic order does not, whatever else, occur in the historical non-space of American "Nature."

The black albino women's appearance in the *Notes* needs to be read in the context of Jefferson's refusal to think the category of black womanhood, and thus, by extension, against the schema of gender and race which urges this deletion. In Jefferson's analyses of both Euro-American and Native American identity, gender relations are made to function as a template of cultural advancement. That is, Jefferson deduces from the organization of gender relations a culture's proximity to nature's legitimating norms. Thus, in his account, the white man's treatment of the white woman reveals his regard for her "natural equality," while the Native

American man asserts the right of "the stronger sex" to simply "impose on the weaker" (*Notes* 60). Typically, Jefferson cannot quite sustain this specious argument, which runs afoul of its obviously partial construction of "nature"; but what concerns me for the moment is less the instability of what Jefferson claims about gender organization than the simple contrast between his insistence on gender's significance to an analysis of Euro- and Native American identity, and his erasure of gender from the body of the African-American. In his infamous evaluation of Phyllis Wheatley, for instance, whose poetry he cites as evidence of the African-American's deficient achievement, Jefferson speaks only to a racial incapacity for cultural refinement—even though, on his own terms, it would seem only "natural" to inquire whether authorship is an appropriate ambition for *women*. Jefferson's refusal to consider what is proper to black womanhood tacitly acknowledges the white man's delegitimation of patriarchal gender norms in the legal determination of the slave's body: unlike either white or Native American men as Jefferson represents them,[42] black men in slavery do not determine the condition of "their female" (*Notes* 139). It is the white man who exerts ownership of the black female body; and, as Hortense Spillers has argued, given the theft of the black body in slavery, gender as such is no longer proper to it. Always ambivalent, Jefferson sometimes verges on querying the condition of the black man in slavery. For example, he suddenly retreats from the proposition of the black man's inferiority lest "our conclusion . . . degrade a whole race of men from the rank in the scale of beings which their Creator may perhaps have given them" (*Notes* 143). But the dominant impulse of the *Notes* is plainly to occlude the white man's role in the degradation of the "race," in the dispossession of the black man and the black woman alike through their construction as property, and in the displacement of patriarchal gender from black bodies, which at once follows and (retroactively) authorizes this construction.[43] In his account of the African-American, Jefferson omits to consider gender, acknowledging that to pursue the topic is dangerously to implicate himself in the legal and social production of his object of study.

Where the black body is concerned, Jefferson strips away gender, and indeed the marks of culture (or ethnicity) altogether, to produce a kind of seamless and paradoxically illegible object. The burden of Jefferson's account is to dislodge the African-American from the symbolic into the realm of objects by demonstrating his natural incapacity for (self-)reflection. Jefferson alternately insists on the black man's inability to produce anything "above the level of plain narration," and cites the black writer Ignatius Sancho for a "wild and extravagant" imagination which "escapes incessantly from every restraint of reason and taste, and, in the course of its vagaries, leaves a tract of thought as incoherent and eccentric, as is the course of a meteor through the sky" (*Notes* 140). The yearning simply to dispose of the black subject drives both representations of the black man's language as strictly literal or entirely non-referential: the point in either case is the black man's inherent incapacity for rational abstraction. However, in representing the black man's language as either marginal (a "plain" iteration of events) or unintelligible, Jefferson flattens him out, reduces him to a mere surface, fully opened to the white man's gaze, but indecipherable: "Are not the fine mixtures of red and white," Jefferson asks, "the expressions of every passion by greater of less suffusions of colour in the one, preferable to the eternal monotony, which reigns in the countenances, that immoveable veil of black, that covers all the emotions of the other race?" (*Notes* 138). Implicit in this ostensibly rhetorical query is both the desire to seal the black body in blackness, to prevent the black man's self-signification, and the fear and revulsion of the radical alterity such a blackout engenders.

In order to mitigate the anxiety that the wholly affectless black body induces—does the veil of blackness conceal the black man's lack, or his presence, his capacity to contest the master's title?—Jefferson ambiguously imparts to black men and women a potential for gendered affect. Jefferson's attempt to naturalize the black body's forced ungendering moves at the same time to (re)contain the black body within a logic of Euro-American gender. In a strangely conceived formulation, Jefferson returns proprietorship of the black woman to the black man, in order to demonstrate how the black man's own sexed nature delegitimates his claim to patriarchal masculinity. While in Jefferson's analysis the black man's sexuality unmans him, gender nevertheless becomes, for the moment, a template of the condition of the race: black men are "more ardent after their female," Jefferson remarks, "but love seems with them to be more an eager desire, than a tender delicate mixture of sentiment and sensation" (*Notes* 139). Alluding to black men's want of "tender . . sentiment" toward "their female," Jefferson implicitly assigns a feminine affectivity to the black "female," whom we must therefore understand as eliciting such "delicacy"; masculine consideration becomes, in this phrasing, the black woman's "natural" due. By feminizing the black woman, Jefferson borders on exposing the thing that will not bear scrutiny: the white man's relation to the black woman and/as a history of violation.[44] Inasmuch as her claim to "tender . . . sentiment" transforms the black "female" into a woman, the white man's institutionalized rape of the black female turns from a legalized property relation into a contingent power relation (unsanctioned by natural law).

If Jefferson wanders between the poles of reducing the black body to the status of a radically unknowable object, or reinvesting it with a destabilizing gendered affectivity, the portrait of the black albino women speaks to and amplifies both impulses. I cite it here in full.

> To this catalogue of our indigenous animals, I will add a short account of an anomaly of nature, taking place sometimes in the race of negroes brought from Africa, who, though black themselves, have in rare instances, white children, called Albinos. I have known four of these myself, and have faithful accounts of three others. The circumstances in which all the individuals agree are these. They are of a pallid cadaverous

white, untinged with red, without any coloured spots or seams; their hair of the same kind of white, short, coarse, and curled as is that of the negro; all of them well formed, strong, healthy, perfect in their senses, except that of sight, and born of parents who had no mixture of white blood. Three of these Albinos were sisters, having two other full sisters, who were black. The youngest of the three was killed by lightning, at twelve years of age. The eldest died at about 27 years of age, in child-bed, with her second child. The middle one is now alive in health, and has issue, as the eldest had, by a black man, which issue was black. They are uncommonly shrewd, quick in their apprehensions and in reply. Their eyes are in a perpetual tremulous vibration, very weak, and much affected by the sun; but they see better in the night than we do. They are of the property of Col. Skipworth, of Cumberland. The fourth is a negro woman, whose parents came from Guinea, and had three other children, who were of their own colour. She is freckled, her eye-sight so weak that she is obliged to wear a bonnet in the summer; but it is better in the night than day. She had an Albino child by a black man. It died at the age of a few weeks. These were the property of Col. Carter, of Albemarle. A sixth instance is a woman of the property of Mr. Butler, near Peters-burgh. She is stout and robust, has issue a daughter, jet black, by a black man. I am not informed as to her eye sight. The seventh instance is of a male belonging to Mr. Lee, of Cumberland. His eyes are tremulous and weak. He is of tall stature, and now advanced in years. He is the only male of the Albinos which have come within my information. Whatever be the cause of the disease in the skin, or in its colouring matter, which produces this change, it seems more incident to the female than male sex. To these I may add the mention of a negro man within my own knowledge, born black, of black parents; on whose chin, when a boy, a white spot appeared. This continued to increase till he became a man, by which time it had extended over his chin, lips, one cheek, the under jaw and neck on that side. It is of the Albino white, without any mixture of red, and has for several years been stationary. He is robust and healthy, and the change of colour was not accompanied with any sen-sible disease, either general or topical. (*Notes* 70-71)

On the black albino body, race undergoes a radical derationali-zation; black albinoism may be read here as the production of whiteness from "out of" blackness. In this frame, blackness exceeds its legal determination, as that which follows solely from the condition of the mother.[45] Thus, in order to authenticate the existence of the black albino—to disallow the common explanation for the origin of the light-skinned slave—Jefferson must introduce a prohibited genealogy into his account of the black albino body. Only by addressing the question of paternity, and permitting black fatherhood to signify, can Jefferson allay the suspicion that these black "albinos" are no more than the peculiar progeny of a white father and a black mother. To identify the body that is neither white, nor black, but non/white is to document an identity systematically erased from the body of the captive black. The non/white subject is defined in terms of the black kinship structures which are at the same time lost to her by virtue of her continuing status as property—the identity of her owner remains as important as her parentage to Jefferson's authentication of the black albino's existence.

Simultaneously constituted as a nameless (numbered) commodity and a social subject (within an illicit black kinship system), the black albino woman accedes, but only partially, to a gendered identity—which she thereby renders visible in its partiality, as a posited or constructed category. This effect is perhaps most striking in the case of the fourth woman Jefferson describes. Pale, freckled, shielded with a bonnet from the sun, the fitting subject for the cameo or miniature over which the sons and daughters of sentimental fiction shed their abundant tears, she poses in a gender of which her "blackness" divests her. In contrast to the non/white man, whose patchwork body appears in barely stabilized flux, the fourth albino woman remains frozen in a posture of affecting frailty. But her identification with the permanence of the liminal white mother, a figure always beyond the operation of history and representation, only speaks to the temporal loss of her child even before its death, as to the loss of herself and her mate, all "the property of Col. Carter." Acceding to a white feminine affect, the fourth woman delegitimates the theft of her body, her child's body, and its father's; at the same time, her accession to maternal affectivity denaturalizes white motherhood. The ineffable expression of the sentimental mother here becomes a transgressive look, a contestatory corporeal style. On the boundary between woman and object, mother and breeder, she historicizes "womanhood" and/as the text of her (un)making. Signifying against the grain of a rational "account[ing]," she gives us her/story in pieces.

2 Charlotte Temple's Remains

The "we" of the declaration [of independence]
speaks "in the name of the people." But this
people does not exist. They do *not* exist as an
entity, it does *not* exist, *before* this declaration,
not as *such*. If it gives birth to itself, as free and
independent subject, as possible signer, this
can hold only in the act of the signature. The
signature invents the signer. This signer can only
authorize him or herself to sign once he or she
has come to the end [parvenu au vout], if one can
say this, of his or her own signature, in a sort of
fabulous retroactivity.
　　　　　—Jacques Derrida

[The] melodramatic weepie is the genre
that seems to endlessly repeat our melancholic
sense of the loss of origins—impossibly hoping
to return to an earlier state which is perhaps
most fundamentally represented by the body of
the mother.
　　　　　—Linda Williams

Some time after the publication of Susanna Rowson's popular novel *Charlotte Temple* (1791), a tombstone inscribed with the
title character's name was erected in Trinity Churchyard in New
York City. If, as Leslie Fiedler suggests, a certain Charlotte Stanley
furnished the inspiration for Rowson's sentimental heroine, the
grave of Charlotte's embodied original had no attraction for the

novel's readers, who flocked instead to Charlotte Temple's tomb, to the extra-textual marker of this textual body's remains.[1] Indeed, for a more than a century they littered the gravesite with locks of hair, ashes of love letters and flowers, and in the words of one late nineteenth-century witness to the scene, kept "the turf over Charlotte Temple . . . fresh with falling tears."[2]

But what exactly should we say has been interred beneath this monument—what kind of body inhabits Charlotte Temple's grave? With this gesture of memorialization, the builders of the grave simultaneously *retrieve* a body from the text and mark its *loss*. By encrypting Charlotte, they produce her body as lost; in other words, they site a body in excess of its discursive articulations, but only as the object of the mourners' melancholic identification. This chapter will read *Charlotte Temple* from the vantage of the churchyard scene in order to interrogate the novel's production of this pre- or post-textual body, and the nonlinear temporality in which its fabrication of an "original" Charlotte transpires.

The epigraphs to this chapter should suggest the political and cultural context(s) in which the novel's temporality interests me. On the one hand, I align *Charlotte Temple* with what Linda Williams identifies as the constitutive belatedness of melodrama, and the phantasm of origins it inscribes on the maternal body.[3] In this respect, the temporality of my own analysis is prospective, locating *Charlotte Temple* in relation to a genre that—particularly in its nondramatic inflection, as the sentimental novel—flourishes in the United States toward the middle of the nineteenth century. On the other hand, I move to juxtapose *Charlotte Temple* and indeed, by implication, the temporality of nineteenth and twentieth century melodrama, with what Jacques Derrida has termed the "fabulous retroactivity" of democratic foundation; with a logic of political legitimation that makes "the people" at once the *justification* for and the *result* of national autonomy; with a practice of textual self-invention that negates the historical contingency of the new political order.[4] I want to suggest how melodrama's commemoration of the loss of origins might be read, not only as itself rehearsing a certain foundationalist logic, but also as contesting the founders' disavowal of history.

Charlotte Temple recovers the alterity of history—history as the possibility of alternative futures—in the form of what has been lost. Specifically, the novel makes visible the existence of those dominant class interests which pre-exist and inform the construction of "the people." It identifies as a class the white, property-owning men whose particular interests the founding texts of the United States make over into "the general interest"—and thus wrenches the category of the "general" from their grasp.[5] In this context, Derrida's equivocation about the gender of the self-emancipating signer is astonishing: by equivocating on this point, he reconstitutes the very fable he is in the process of undoing and legitimates the fiction of the signer's spontaneous self-generation. His equivocation thus participates in the erasure of the history of pre-existing social relations that determine who accedes to the status of signatory in the first place. These pre-existing relations establish the white man's privilege as signer, his self-abstraction as a metonymy of "the people" in whose name he signs; and conversely, the existing structure of power is determining for the status of non-male and non-white bodies as hopelessly particularized, inadequate to the function of signatory, or citizen, because irreducible to the white masculine generic.[6] I will argue that Charlotte Temple at once acknowledges and resists this cultural logic of representation that renders white middle-class women unrepresentative of "the general interest." To the extent that it resists, the novel (re)constitutes them as a political body—which is to say that it retraces the limits of the representable.

The novel reflects on its own transgressive project in the form of an ostensibly positivist claim to historical authenticity. Although the subtitle to Charlotte Temple, "A Tale of Truth," functions most obviously to defend against the moralist's conventional accusation—that the novel as a genre glamorized seduction—it serves more subtly to redefine the possibilities of representing women in an order that denies their political representability. Contemporary criticism of the novel hinged on the juxtaposition of its pernicious influence on the female reader to the benign effects of historical reading. As critics such as Benjamin Rush and Timothy Dwight contended, this impressionable reader would be unable to distance herself from the examples of fallen womanhood she encountered in the novel form. "What can the reader expect," laments Dwight, "after having resided so long in novels, but that fortunes, and villas, and Edens, will spring up every where in her progress through life, to promote her enjoyment. She has read herself into a heroine, and is fairly entitled to all the appendages of this character."[7] On the contrary, immoral feminine conduct as represented in historical narratives effectively deterred the reader from emulation. Thus when Mercy Otis Warren, echoing these male authorities on the subject of female education, exhorts women to put aside all "books that have not a tendency to instill lessons of virtue," she goes on in the same breath to enjoin the reading of "authentic history, which is now written in a style equally elegant to the many volumes of romance, which in the present age croud around the public."[8]

While in one sense Rowson's assertion of the novel's historicity concedes to its moral critics "authentic history['s]" superiority, in another sense it contests their alignment of representable femininity with the singular historical figure, with the woman whose very place in the historical record attests to her eccentricity. If a historical model for Charlotte existed, then she was, like Charlotte, marked out precisely by her lack of singularity, by her resemblance to a character in a seduction novel, her status as a *generic* figure. Leslie Fiedler observes as much about the historical Charlotte Stanley, on whom Rowson was said to have modelled her heroine, quipping that the author of *Clarissa* had of course "invented . . . [Charlotte Stanley's] life before she managed to live it."[9] Insofar as the paradigmatic Charlotte has been divested of the historical woman's distinctiveness, Rowson's claim to historical authenticity remains disingenuous: Charlotte's "tale" is "true," but only because "truth" now lies outside Dwight's ideology of history. Rather than claim morality for the novel, Rowson moves to establish a competing pedagogical code.

As in fact the churchyard spectacle suggests, Charlotte compels the very attachment Dwight attributes to the seduction novel's heroine, if not precisely for the reasons he identifies. While Dwight looks to the material pleasures of a kept woman's existence to explain the reader's attraction to a woman such as Charlotte, an attraction, he seems to surmise, that cannot be explained in terms of her vacuous character, I argue to the contrary that Charlotte's flatness, her merely generic femininity, allows her to stand in for the novel's readership, makes her (the) representative of this diffuse body of white middle-class female readers. The graveside mourners refuse to sever their affective ties to the fallen Charlotte, as indeed the moralist argues that they must, not because they have invested her with the aura of social privilege, but because she invests them with a collective identity.

Judith Butler's reading of gender as masquerade offers a particularly compelling model for understanding the mourners' relation to Charlotte. Masquerade functions in her account, not to conceal a primary or essential identity, but to preserve by way of incorporation a connection that must be refused:

> The mask has a double function which is the double function of melancholy. The mask is taken on through the process of incorporation which is a way of inscribing and then wearing a melancholic identification in and on the body; in effect, it is the signification of the body in the mold of the Other who has been refused. Dominated through appropriation, every refusal fails, and the refuser becomes part of the very identity of the refused, indeed, becomes the psychic refuse of the refused. The loss of the object is never absolute because it is redistributed within a psychic/corporeal boundary that expands to incorporate that loss.[10]

As the mark of the loss that it serves to occlude, the mask constitutes the gendered subject in the image of the lost object/other. In this frame, we might recast the mourners' refusal to repudiate their bond to Charlotte as their "domination through appropriation" of their political loss(es).[11] Through their melancholic identification with Charlotte, the mourners reconfigure themselves psychically and corporeally in the image of what the law refuses white middle-class women, in the image of the juridical and political identity that they lack. The mourners thus render themselves representable, but only to other readers of the sentimental seduction tale. If the ruse of identity is its apparent inherence in the individual subject, the mourners' feminine identity here becomes contingent on their mutual recognition of its text. For the novel's melancholy reader, gendered identity is experienced as a social relation.

All the Appendages of Character?

In the opening portions of the novel, Rowson rehearses the circumstances of Charlotte's mother's marriage to the young Mr. Temple. This narrative of Lucy's passage from her father's to her husband's house elaborates a model of normative femininity against which Charlotte's fall from virtue is to be read. Yet Lucy represents more than the ideal of early republican womanhood, of a domesticated, or privatized femininity; her narrative suggests further the way in which white middle-class republican woman-hood is wholly assimilated to the space of the private, assumes the burden of interiority as such for the bourgeois subject and by extension in and for the dominant culture as a whole.[12] In other words, Lucy not only *has* feelings, but she embodies bourgeois feeling *in general*. She is *normative* in the very fact of her *excessive* capacity for sentiment, for the display of inner life that sustains the fiction of exteriority—of autonomous masculinity, national identity, the public sphere. We first encounter Lucy, having lost her mother and brother in a series of calamitous misfortunes, voicing the desire to expire with her father. "Oh my father," she exclaims when he seeks to discuss her future, "daily are my prayers offered to heaven that our lives may terminate at the same instant, and one grave receive us both; for why should I live when deprived of my only friend?"[13] If Lucy remains otherwise mute in the novel's early chapters, her pathetic attachment to a shattered domestic scene—her single, hyperbolic assertion that she can have no existence on the *outside,* outside the private sphere of affective relations—does not go unnoticed: enchanted with this outpouring of derelict feminine sentiment, Temple moves immediately to house it, to appropriate it in a new familial configuration, or a "Temple" to democratic sociality.

Even before the pantomimic exchange of glances that constitutes her courtship, it is inevitable that Lucy will consent to this union. Moved to tears by Lucy's plight, Temple rescues her destitute father from the debtor's prison where he has been confined. While Temple is certainly not guilty of mere self-interest in this affair—in discharging the father's heavy burden of debt, he depletes his fortune and restricts his own social prospects—sentiment plainly flows along the channels of economic dependencies. Thus Temple can anticipate with apparent propriety and self-assurance the "exquisite transport [it will be] to see the expressive eyes of Lucy beaming at once with pleasure for her father's deliverance, and gratitude for her deliverer" (*CT* 21). By predicating Lucy's sentiments toward him on their economic affiliation, Temple imposes the logic of coverture, the principle of republican law—imported, via the British legal tradition, from feudal France—that submerges the wife's legal and economic identity in her husband's, a legal principle that doubles as the (historical) justification for women's political invisibility and its (naturalized) effect. If coverture follows marriage, Temple reasons, marriage should follow coverture. In short order, Temple thus acquires in his own name Lucy's affecting feminine presence, who now assumes her properly reproductive social function. It is in her capacity as what Linda Kerber has termed "the Republican Mother" that the privatized/covered woman emerges as a force (if not exactly an agent) for socialization.[14] Refused political participation, denied her title to property or the right to function in any contractual relation independently of her husband, the white middle-class woman functions to reproduce the order that effaces her. As an absent (unrepresentable) presence, she signifies precisely the possibilities or prospects *lost* to the child in its accession to subjectivity; the mother occupies the position of the not-(yet-)subject. Newly and vividly celebrated in early national culture, this mother-child relation thus concerns less the child's relation to a specific (maternal) subject than the child's relation to its own rational subjectivity. Specifically, *Charlotte Temple* suggests, it is in the register of a maternal love which knows no bounds that the child is subordinated to rational identity as the limit of cultural intelligibility—a limit the child thus internalizes at the point of *affectively* exceeding it.

> Oh my friends, as you value your eternal happiness, wound not, by thoughtless ingratitude, the peace of the mother who bore you: remember the tenderness, the care, the unremitting anxiety with which she has attended to all your wants and wishes from earliest infancy to the present day; behold the mild ray of affectionate applause that beams from her eye on the performance of your duty; listen to her reproofs with silent attention; they proceed from a heart anxious for your future felicity: you must love her; nature, all-powerful nature, has planted the seeds of filial affection in your bosoms.
>
> Then once more read over the sorrows of poor Mrs. Temple, and remember, the mother whom you so dearly love and venerate will feel the same, when you, forgetful of the respect due your maker and yourself, forsake the paths of virtue for those of vice and folly. (*CT* 54)

Here we find the maternal injunction to observe rational social form emitted—rather than articulated—in a beam of "affectionate" affirmation. Likewise, the mother's moral "reproofs" (the discourse of the proper) flow (in an affecting breach of good form) from the heart. Maternal love becomes the medium of the child's interpellation in the social, because it is also the medium in which the partiality of the rational subject is disavowed. For the daughter to fall from virtue, to fail in the performance of her duty, is in Rowson's description not simply, or not so much, to disappoint her mother, understood as a person, complexly situated *within* the social. Rather, as the novel suggests, to disappoint maternal love is to fall *from* the social—to fall into a state of abjection.[15] Charlotte's fall from middle-class respectability terminates not in a lower-class identity, in a diminished social privilege, but in the dissolution of her identity altogether.

Yielding to the seducer Montraville, Charlotte "falls a victim to her too great sensibility"; falls victim, in other words, to her own femininity, to an unlimited capacity for sentiment. If femininity in this historical context signifies a radical form of being-for-another, signifies service as the embodied site of the other's self-elaboration, then the daughter seems generically predisposed to waywardness. Seduction is criminal not because it involves the dissipation of feminine personality (to be a woman is to inhabit the dimension of diffusive sympathies), but because it circumvents the institutions (of family; marriage) that regulate (cover; interiorize) the flow of feminine affect. Outside such institutional matrices, Charlotte simply vanishes—in succumbing to Montraville's pleas, resigns even the power to succumb:

> "I cannot go," said she: "cease, dear Montraville, to persuade. I must not: religion, duty, forbid."
> "Cruel Charlotte," said he, "if you disappoint my ardent hopes, by all that is sacred, this hand shall put a period to my existence. I cannot—will not live without you."
> "Alas! my torn heart!" said Charlotte, "how shall I act?"
> "Let me direct you," said Montraville, lifting her into the chaise.
> "Oh! my dear forsaken parents!" cried Charlotte.
> The chaise drove off. She shrieked, and fainted into the arms of her betrayer. (*CT* 47-48)

If this depiction of Charlotte's flight as something between an abduction and an elopement recalls the germinal *Clarissa,* unlike Richardson, Rowson brackets the question of Charlotte's agency altogether.[16] Charlotte is carried off neither against, nor in accordance with her will; once she softens to Montraville's pathetic appeal, she has no will to assert, no power to concur or to dissent.

Uncovered and seduced from her father's protection into the embrace of a man who has neither the means nor the intention to domesticate her, Charlotte can no longer be spoken of in relation to the forms of rationalized sociality. What remains on the scene is not so much a character, and even less a caricature, but a figure of pure affect, uncovered, freed and abject.

As she sobs, faints and convulses her way through the cruel twists of a wayward daughter's fate, Charlotte exasperates both the literary critic with a taste for subtle characterization and psychological verisimilitude, and, Rowson insinuates, the consumer of sentimental fiction herself: "'Bless my heart,' cries my young, volatile reader, 'I shall never have patience to get through these volumes, there are so many ahs! and ohs! so much fainting, tears, and distress, I am sick to death of the subject'" (*CT* 98). Yet Rowson goes on to solicit her reader's patience under the banner, precisely, of truth in the novel: ". . my lively, innocent girl, I must request your patience: I am writing a tale of truth: I mean to write it to the heart: but if perchance the heart is rendered impenetrable by unbounded prosperity, or a continuance in vice, I expect not my tale to please, nay I even expect it will be thrown by with disgust" (*CT* 99). To the reader who protests the apparent banality of Charlotte's engagement with the world, that makes each scene in which she figures a repetition of the last, Rowson responds that the "truth of the tale" is vested exactly in the interminable series of affective moments of which Charlotte's history is comprised. In order to appreciate the tale, Rowson urges, the young female reader must think beyond virtuous indignation or vicious derision: she must think as a woman (think beyond moral form) and melt in sympathy for Charlotte. It is the mark of the moralist and the harlot alike (of the "sober matron" with whom Rowson engages in her asides to the reader, as well as of the wilfully licentious La Rue, who masterminds Charlotte's elopement with Montraville) to recoil in revulsion from Charlotte's uncovered feminine presence. If covered feminine affect underwrites rational subject formation, uncovered feminine affect *reverts* to the white middle-class woman, as the register of her own relation to the social and to democratic representational forms. By affectively participating in Charlotte's dissolution, the reader comes to feel for herself—in both possible meanings of the phrase.

In other words, the melting sympathy for Charlotte of those readers whom Rowson distinguishes from the censuring matron and the hardened offender as "my dear girls," releases them from a state of rationalized non-identity into a derationalized sociality. Furthermore, in this context Charlotte's pregnancy, though anything but unexpected, marks a critical turn in the narrative. The affective bond which binds the reader to this (expectant) mother works, precisely, to attenuate the reader's connection to the normative forms of democratic sociality. As Charlotte moves from girlhood into motherhood, she assumes the full disruptive power of the negative exemplum; if maternal affect in the covered woman is the medium of rational subject formation, in the outcast the moral imperative is stripped away from the face of maternal sentiment.

In the eyes of the stalwart republican, the helpless Charlotte, destitute and nearing her confinement, is therefore a spectacle to freeze the blood and turn the heart to stone. "Alas poor Charlotte," Rowson comments on her heroine's vain appeal to a crude landlady's sympathy, "how confined was her knowledge of human nature . . . for when once the petrifying aspect of distress and penury appear, whose qualities, like Medusa's head, can change to stone all that look upon it; when once this Gorgon claims acquaintance with us, the phantom of friendship, that before courted our notice, will vanish into unsubstantial air, and the whole world before us appears a barren waste" (*CT* 102). In her "distress and penury," as the outcast mother-to-be, the abject Charlotte acquires Medusa's deadly aspect, assumes the emblematic form of the monstrous reproductive body. If the working-class landlady is proof against the spectacle, discerning in Charlotte only the laughable posturings of a leisured woman, Mademoiselle La Rue, on the other hand, bound to Charlotte by class as well as gender affinity, fully perceives the monstrous possibilities of uncovered repro-

duction: "Take her away," she cries, when the homeless Charlotte
turns up in search of a place to bear her child, "she will really
frighten me into hysterics; take her away I say this instant . . . , Any
where, only don't let me ever see her again" (CT 109).

Reading Herself into a Heroine

La Rue's double betrayal, her inability to endure the spectacle
she has herself engendered, ultimately forecloses on one possible
narrative outcome, in which Charlotte's fall would be termi-
nated—she would assume a *position* as a fallen woman—and the
flow of readerly tears would abate. But the flaunter of morals defines herself by the same standards as the moralist, Charlotte discovers, and comments, judiciously for once, "this is too much"
(CT 108). Ironically, La Rue justifies her dismissal of Charlotte's
pathetic request for shelter by invoking the proprieties of wedded
life. Legitimately connected now to the gullible Mr. Crayton, who
learns too late of his wife's markedly unsympathetic bent, La Rue
insists that she could neither afford to impugn her own reputation
by seeming to condone the dissipated life of a woman such as
Charlotte, nor would she risk incurring for her husband the expense of Charlotte's care. This travesty of feminine morals, La Rue's
feigned appreciation of the wife's imputed moral role, inaugurates
the narration of Charlotte's labor, delirium, and death. While republican assumptions about feminine identity come under open
censure in this scene, in which the language of domestic sensibility speaks its own condemnation in the mouth of the hypocrite,
Charlotte begins to apprehend as her *own* this feminine capacity
for sympathy, which overflows the constitutive divisions of a
rationalized social space (inside/outside, private/public). In the
interstice between her social and her bodily decomposition,
Charlotte comes to identify with the abject mother she halluci-
nates in her feverish state.

Realizing that she is pregnant and that Montraville's feelings for
her have died, Charlotte begs her parents to abet her return, and

recounts in a letter a recurrent dream in which her father first, and then her mother, reproach her for her mother's murder:

> At other times I see my father angry and frowning, point to horrid caves, where on the cold damp ground, in the agonies of death, I see my dear mother and my revered grand-father. I strive to raise you; you push me from you, and shrieking cry—"Charlotte, thou hast murdered me!" Horror and despair tear every tortured nerve; I start, and leave my restless bed. . . . (*CT* 81)

In the initial realization of her own impending motherhood, Charlotte relives her separation from her mother as a murder, as a violent rupture enacted on the primal ground of "horrid caves." Thus she seems at once to invest this separation from her mother with the painful intensity of parturition, which spares the guilty child in this case and kills the mother, and to imagine that in her own maternal body is taking form only the empty horror of a broken connection. The peculiarity of the scene, however, which at once underscores and complicates the symbolism of this encounter, is the presence of the grandfather, sharing her mother's pain rather than her father's ire. Yet this distribution is central, I would suggest, to Charlotte's symbolization of her motherhood as a rift, as the deadly severance of affective ties: the grandfather's presence in the cave serves to locate Charlotte's experience of loss within the terms of coverture, and more particularly within the construction of motherhood as moral tuition that coverture promotes. If the grandfather comes to occupy the same position as his daughter in the dream, the logic of their pairing is economic; when Temple acquires Lucy as a source of familial affect, he acquires her father in the bargain. Unable to protect either his daughter or his own interest, the grandfather, too, assumes the identity of Temple's dependent, and consequently that of a feminized medium of sentiment in Temple's domestic order. Insofar as sentimental attachment is governed by the logic of economic dependencies, then, Charlotte's alienation from her mother appears to be of the same order as her alienation from this emasculated patriarch.

Charlotte's vision of her wounded mother recurs with a difference after the birth of her daughter, whom Charlotte initially refuses to acknowledge as her own:

> "Oh," said she one day, starting up on hearing the infant cry, "why, why will you keep that child here; I am sure you would not if you knew how hard it was for a mother to be parted from her infant: it is like tearing the cords of life asunder. Oh could you see the horrid sight which I now behold—there—there stands my dear mother, her poor bosom bleeding at every vein, her gentle, affectionate heart torn in a thousand pieces, and all for the loss of a ruined, ungrateful child. Save me—save me—from her frown. I dare not—indeed I dare not speak to her." (*CT* 111)

The grandfather no longer figures in this version of Charlotte's dream, and the bleeding mother herself appears to have assumed the father's censuring gaze. But the mother no longer voices her reproach; it is Charlotte in her terror who attributes anger to this "gentle, affectionate" figure, a figure which appears to have transcended, through the anguish of its rent and bleeding heart, through its own slow dissolution, the imperative to moral judgment altogether—it is Charlotte, in short, who sees a "Gorgon" where there is none and recoils in panic from its frown. In fact, the mother's appearance here has assumed all the characteristic marks of Charlotte's own, so that in facing this image of abject womanhood Charlotte faces herself, and the terms of her own motherhood as well.

Charlotte's vision here anticipates the tender recognition of her child in the scene that follows. By displacing herself in this vision between the infant's position—in her delirium, she sees her crying child as parted from its mother, like herself—and the mother's, Charlotte realizes a continuity between Lucy Temple, her daughter, and herself. She uncovers a sentimental affiliation that obtains despite her displacement from the privatized domain of feminine feeling and that finds its inscription in her child's name: little Lucy restores the broken connection between Charlotte and her mother and reveals a maternal succession that operates independently of legitimated genealogies. Significantly, when some years after Charlotte's death, an aging La Rue, left destitute by the wages of sin, comes for relief to Charlotte's parents' door, the child that bears Lucy's name shows Charlotte's face. "Heaven have mercy!" La Rue moans, gazing at little Lucy, "I see her [Charlotte] now" (CT 119).

In articulating Charlotte's unbroken connection to her mother, a connection that establishes a ground, in turn, for Charlotte's accession to motherhood, Rowson engages the possibility of signifiable relations between women: by uncovering the maternal sympathies that bind Lucy to her fallen daughter and the daughter's illegitimate child, Rowson models a derationalized affective relation. Inasmuch as the young female reader, Rowson's "dear young girl," maintains her melancholic attachment to Charlotte, she enters into this counter-familial affiliation; like little Lucy, she styles herself in Charlotte's image. The identification of Charlotte's readers with her daughter is in fact suggested in the novel: "if my child should be a girl," Charlotte instructs her parents, ". . . tell her the unhappy fate of her mother" (CT 81). Lucy herself, then, like the consumer of this fiction, is imagined as a product of her mother's tale. Little Lucy's resemblance to her mother, melodramatically acknowledged by La Rue, thus anticipates and thematizes the readers' incorporation of the novel's fallen heroine.

The Pensioner of Friendship

It is arguably in response to Rowson's projection of a middle-class women's community that Hannah Foster attempts in her novel *The Coquette*—which followed the first American edition of *Charlotte Temple* by just three years—to represent such a collective, to signify relations between women in the ambiguously (de)privatized zone of "friendship." Unlike Rowson, whose historical model for Charlotte—if indeed she had one—never interested her readers, Foster took as her pattern for Eliza Wharton a notorious figure named Elizabeth Whitman, whose death in childbirth in a

Connecticut tavern, with neither family nor friends in attendance, had been a well-publicized scandal.[17] So Eliza Wharton's tale opens, symbolically at least, on the scene of Elizabeth Whitman's grave—opens, one might say, where *Charlotte Temple* leaves off, on the affecting image of its heroine's tombstone. The readers' perception of Eliza is thus, in one sense, always retrospective—always already a function Elizabeth Whitman's loss.[18] Yet it is precisely the re-presentation of this loss that the narrative seeks to defer, by placing the community of (potential) mourners within the text, in the form of myriad sympathizing friends, who labor to deflect Eliza's textual reenactment of Elizabeth's fate. In this frame, Foster may be seen to operate on the model of Derrida's founders, who author(ize) themselves by disavowing the contingency of their textual self-production, by strategically forgetting their pre-texts. Significantly, then, the better portion of *The Coquette* is concerned, not with the narration of Eliza'a fall—of her illicit trysts with Sanford, her concealed pregnancy, midnight elopement, and death—but with her determined attempt to maintain her status as *feme sole,* neither married nor under parental protection, among the community of her middle-class, white, female friends.

Throughout most of the novel, Eliza operates in a state of suspension, poised between Charlotte's and Elizabeth's realized fate and her own imminent fall, and claiming, in this state, the right to what she calls her "freedom," and her devoted though skeptical friends refer to as "a play about words."[19] Eliza attempts, in short, the divorce of sympathy from the constraints of the privatized domestic sphere, envisions her power to feel, not as the medium of social interpellation, but as the medium of social relations between women. Paradoxically, however, in her attempt at independence, Eliza must rely on the hospitality of her *married* women friends; she must become, as she puts it, "a pensioner of friendship" in their domestic realms (*CQ* 36). As an uncovered feminine presence occupying a kind of social non-space—living under the protection, the coverture, as it were, of women who, being themselves covered, have no protection to extend—Eliza forms a middle-class women's community with neither social nor economic legitimacy, engenders an identity that cuts across the division of private and public space, turning the feminine inside out.

Dependent on the alienation, or at least the partial alienation of Eliza's covered "protectors" from the terms of their coverture, this illegitimate body is quickly dismembered. While she lives, and principally, while she still asserts her right to unrestricted sentimental communion, Eliza finds her sphere of influence progressively diminished as "the pleasing scenes of domestic life" (*CQ* 97), and, in particular, the duties of motherhood, claim the attention of her most sympathetic hosts. Foster's attempt to locate Eliza in the temporality of the founder's political self-invention, in the arrested time of a declaration that reinvents the conditions of its own possibility, yields to the recognition of existing social relations, which render relations between women unrepresentable. Eliza's power to incorporate her women friends remains contingent on her replication of Elizabeth's fate. In the closing moments of the novel, at the limits of the narrative as it were, her fall reintegrates this dismembered body as a body of mourners, which forms again around the locus of an absence, (re)assembles around a grave.

For all its grounding in "authentic history," its apparent concession to the terms of republican moral instruction, *The Coquette* is a tale about the "truth" of the early American seduction tale. Foster's attempt to represent a community of (at least partially) uncovered women, centered symbolically on this affecting *feme sole,* works to demonstrate the unrepresentability of republican women's social and political affinities. Reading *The Coquette,* we are reminded that Rowson constitutes such a community in mourning, as the mark of a prohibition on *Charlotte Temple's* melancholy readers. The political identity of republican women—of those women belonging to an ascendent bourgeoisie—enters national life in the form of an incorporated loss, enshrined and negated, like the fictional Charlotte Temple's remains.

3 Revivification and Utopian Time

Poe versus Stowe

It is only the utopian in some archetypes that
enables their fruitful citation when looking
forward, not backward. That has already
occurred in the apparent interlocking of the
phantasmagorias and in the dissolution of that
appearance. All those rationalisms concerning
mothers, *as those who are still giving birth,* show
a light shining in from utopia, even during
romanticism with the yearning graves and
underworld lantern. The particular brooding
in archetypes, and especially that, shows their
incompleteness.

　　　　—Ernst Bloch

Bloch's remark about mothers, appended apparently by way
of example to a discussion of the utopian components in certain
archetypes, puts several terms into play: on the one hand, something he calls "rationalisms" of motherhood, associated here with a
"utopian light"; on the other hand, the "phantasmagorias," or arche-
typal images, of the gothic romance.[1] Bloch fails to elucidate this
odd configuration of terms. But in the very linking of "rationalisms"
to gothicism (incidental as the locution "even during" makes their
historical relation appear), a useful (re)construction of his elliptical
allusion to motherhood emerges. The development of the gothic
as a cultural genre in the late eighteenth and early nineteenth
centuries intersects with a specifically modern rationalization of

motherhood, one that participates in the Enlightenment project of rationalizing the social body. In this construction of motherhood, as I have argued, the mother becomes the mediator of democratic social and political forms, the producer of the rational citizen. The identification of the white middle-class mother with the social, to which her legal and political visibility is sacrificed, arguably engenders the antithetical and complementary excesses of the gothic, the imagery of subterranean maternal presence, of the "yearning grave." This kinship, or historical convergence, of the rationalized and the phantasmatic, of the socially reproductive mother and the not quite (not sufficiently) dead occupant of the "yearning grave," reveals itself decisively in the discourse of sentimentalism, and its figuration of the Good Christian Mother, as one whose moral influence extends beyond the grave, affecting her children's actions long after she herself is dead.

But where is the "utopian" in the bourgeois mother's (re)production of the rational social body? I insist on the question because it concerns more than the coherence of a particular, cryptic example: Bloch's apparently casual reference to the utopian resonance of the mother's (re)productive role conceals the *centrality* of this maternal function to his conception of a "utopian drive," as he elaborates it throughout *The Utopian Function of Art and Literature*. In Bloch's definition, the utopian drive inheres in particular signifiers that contain in embryo the possibility, or prospect, of difference. The utopian signifier incorporates that which is alien to it, in the form of the not-yet-known, of its "not-worked-through, non-mythical surplus." This "surplus" remains in excess of the signifier's historically delimited meaning, of the false, or merely partial, consciousness this signifier articulates.[2] To cite the "utopian in some archetypes" is to decipher in the archetype a latent, or immanent, alterity. The utopian function is thus organized, or informed, by a metaphorics of gestation: the utopian signifier brings to term within itself the potential form of the other. The "rationalisms concerning mothers, *as those who are still giving birth*," bearing new forms of being within, in fact furnish the conceptual model of the utopian drive; as Bloch conceives it, the "utopian function" is a function of the rationalized maternal body.

Bloch's model for the cultural production of utopia is itself the product of the "rationalisms concerning mothers" which he acknowledges here, but only as an *example* of utopian signification. More precisely, Bloch's model is the product of such "rationalisms" at their point of juncture with the gothic archetype of "the yearning grave," a juncture which I am proposing to locate in the discourse of sentimentalism. By designating this more or less classically Marxist model of cultural production as sentimental,[3] I mean to suggest that Marxist critical discourse reproduces the logic of bourgeois rationalism to the extent that it, too, discovers in the essentialized maternal body the condition of its own transhistorical elaboration.[4] At the same time, I want to (re)read sentimentalism in the frame of Bloch's analysis, as a utopian/political discourse, insofar as its figuration of the Good Christian Mother is pregnant with a radically other possibility. Unlike Bloch, however, I align the good Christian mother's alterity, not with the rationalisms that shed light into the gothic crypt, but with something that at once inhabits and exceeds the rational and the gothic planes of the mother's sentimental portrait. Sentimental discourse can be seen to lead a varied life, as a "rationalism concerning mothers," operating in the service of a rationalized social and political order; as a (gothic) mythology of motherhood, which only reproduces the logic of a rationalized maternity; and finally, as the utopian, or "non-mythical surplus," of the sentimental portrait, where the "incompleteness" of the Good Christian Mother, and of the rational social order, is made legible.

To locate the "non-mythological surplus" of the white middle-class mother in the culture of nineteenth-century democracy is to see, not just beyond her domestication, but beyond her highly *mythologized* excess. The mythologized surplus of bourgeois motherhood arguably finds its privileged articulation in psychoanalysis, which takes up Bloch's rational/gothic binary, to insist both on the mother's absence (her lack) within the social (oedipal motherhood) and on her haunting anteriority (pre-oedipal motherhood). Inasmuch as the utopian component of sentimental motherhood is immanent within, but not reducible to, the imagery of the "yearning grave," however, it is also not reducible to the psychoanalytic decoding of the "yearning grave" as womb, as the edenic space of the mother-infant dyad. The point is that the preoedipal, or pretextual, mother embodies that which is constitutively absent in the speaking subject. To *represent* the pre-oedipal mother, one must be *outside* the dyadic enclosure, so that the representation of maternal origins signifies their loss. While Bloch's utopian prospect is there in what one says, un- or underheard, but always (potentially) enlightening, the maternal body, conceived as origin, is what is *not* there insofar as one is in a position to say anything at all.[5]

In fact, sentimental narrative frequently figures the mother as either dead or dying; she is the iconic absence in and of the sentimental narrative, the cameo, the memory, the deeply affecting, compulsively reproduced image of one who is, literally and symbolically, not of this world. An indelible memory, she haunts her progeny with the recollection of an infantile bliss, marked by her perfectly loving (angelic) presence. The "yearning" of this encrypted mother is socially (re)productive, in the sense that her memory imparts to (recuperates for) the individuated subject a feeling of integrity. In its alignment of rational and gothic motherhood, sentimental discourse offers this insight into democratic sociality: that the domestic angel best accomplishes her mission from the grave, insofar as she is always already a presence under erasure. This sentimental economy of motherhood comes nicely into focus in Margaret Fuller's construction of the mother as moral influence.

> Man is of Woman born, and her face bends over him in infancy with an expression he can never quite forget. Eminent men have delighted to pay tribute to this image. . . . The rudest tar brushes off a tear with his coat-sleeve at the hallowed name. . . . Some gleams of the same expres-

sion which shone down upon his infancy, angelically pure and benign, visit Man again with hopes of pure love, of a holy marriage. Or, if not before, in the eyes of the mother of his child they again are seen, and dim fancies pass before his mind, that Woman may not have been born for him alone, but have come from heaven, a commissioned soul, a messenger of truth and love; that she can only make for him a home in which he may lawfully repose, in so far as she is "True to the kindred points of Heaven and home."

In gleams, in dim fancies, this thought visits the mind of common men. It is soon obscured by the mists of sensuality, the dust of routine, and he thinks it was only some meteor or ignis fatuus that shone. But as a Rosicrucian lamp, it burns unwearied, though condemned to the solitude of tombs.[6]

In a first moment, the mother here embodies the possibility of pre- or non-symbolic "expression"; her face, and metonymically her body, is itself a communication, so replete with meaning for the supine infant that its "message" never fully ceases. In Fuller's mythology, the originary maternal body is naturally or essentially significant—discloses its meanings without recourse to the order of signifiers. But remembering the mother's body, its mute and ineffable "expression," the sentimental "tar" only registers its loss— pays nostalgic tribute to a "hallowed *name*." More precisely, the remembered maternal body in this passage is divested of anything that might mark its "expression" as the mother's own: maternal "expression" becomes the medium of the normative social imagination. Thus the mother's face is now "commissioned," made the bearer of another's message, the purveyor of the Father's truth, casting the sanction of divine authority on the domestic realm. From this perspective, the memory of his dead mother recalls her son to the "truth and love" of paternal law, the benignity of moral limits.

But if on one level, her son's evolving relation to the symbolic determines the mother's status (she is the subject's origin, and not herself a subject), on another level the mother Fuller envisions is something more, or something potentially other, than a recollected "expression" or a "hallowed name." Fuller's unforgettable mother is (also) a *visitation,* a spectral presence, a thing—a possibility—external to the son's psychic and corporeal boundaries. More exactly, this luminous mother is at once internal to the structures of the filial subject (a projection; a mere hallucination), and irreducibly other (an actual ghost). Positioned ambiguously within and without the son's psychic economy, Fuller's spectral mother erodes this limit, to expose the rational subject of democratic representation as a contingent entity, constituted within a complexly intersubjective field.

A "non-mythological surplus" arises from Fuller's portrait of the sentimental mother, something that inhabits but also (prospectively) derationalizes the maternal. A figure emerges in this portrait too present to be identified with the original/pretextual mother (symbolically constituted as absent), and too sensational, too invasive with respect to masculine corporeal boundaries to be identified with the iconic mother (whose remembered "expression" underwrites the integrity of the individuated subject). Rather this emergent figure occupies the fissure between these two mythologized positions, between the pre-rational mother and the domestic angel, and thereby "anticipates," to use Bloch's term, the potential difference of a maternal *subject.* It is not the mother's position in excess of the social and symbolic order—in the Eden of a lost expressiveness—that opens up a utopian perspective in Fuller's portrait of motherhood, but rather the mother's (spectral) existence in the present tense of historical time. This (re)animated mother, arisen from the grave, denaturalizes both pre-rational motherhood (that which is excluded from the social), and domesticated motherhood (that which embodies the social as affect).

If the formulas and set pieces of sentimental fiction are charged with a "non-mythological surplus," their "immanent alterity" arguably finds its expression in the weeping reader. The readers' dissolution in tears of sympathy not only maintains connection to what is lost, but also anticipates the dissolution of a rational subjectivity. Their weeping marks the readers' wordless recognition of the underheard alternative, of a purely prospective yet already affecting difference. Despite what sentimental authors liked to imagine, however, susceptibility to the portrait of ideal motherhood failed to transcend social divisions. In the figure of "the rudest tar," the wizened old sailor moved to tears at his mother's name, Fuller subtly argues for (by celebrating) the universally affecting qualities of sentimental motherhood. But the actual "rudest tar" was most likely no sentimentalist; sentimentalism is a race- and class-bound discourse, grounded in domestic ideology and middle-class family structures. As Christine Stansell has shown, for instance, the working-class women—whom the middle-class consumers of sentimental fiction periodically undertook to redeem—easily intuited that the discourse of sentimentalism couched as Christian charity what remained in fact a mission of "social domination."[7] While the tear of sympathy was *not* the glue that healed all social divisions, that bound together all races and classes, as sentimentalists sometimes sought to claim—while sentimentalism could indeed be made to serve egregiously racist and classist polemics (often in the very rhetoric with which it espoused such causes as abolition)— nevertheless sentimentalism does not reduce to a univocal affirmation of middle-class ideologies.[8]

Interestingly, the sentimental authors' claim for the socially leveling effect of sentimental writing reappears in the lament of modern mass culture critics, such as Ann Douglas, for whom the popularity of the sentimental novel marks a leveling of discursive forms, a "feminization" of United States culture.[9] But strangely, what turns out to have been "feminized," as this argument goes, is not the "high" cultural domain that is traditionally gendered masculine, but a popular discourse *conventionally* associated with effusion and excess. Sentimental fiction's mass circulation thus appears restricted, conveniently, to the "masses" and the masculine preserve of "high" culture, though marginalized, remains intact. If sentimentalism is a feminized discourse, it neither successfully colonizes the entire field of popular culture, nor does it entirely fail to colonize the imagination of a literary elite, composed of white middle- and upper-class male writers. Poe as well as Stowe writes the discourse of sentimentalism—even if, as I aim to show, the politics of "revivification" elide the utopian perspective onto which (re)animation opens.

Poe's "Hideous Drama"

The tale of Ligeia's resurrection, her reincarnation in the body of another, represents, in the narrator's own words, "a hideous drama of revivification," hideous in the insistence of Ligeia's demand for life, a demand articulated in the corporeal idiom of the flush and the tremor, and in the resistance of Rowena's frame to these incursions of being.

> At length it became evident that a slight, a very feeble, and barely noticeable tinge of color had flushed up within the cheeks, and along the sunken small veins of the eyelids. Through a species of unutterable horror and awe, for which the language of mortality has no sufficiently energetic expression, I felt my heart cease to beat, my limbs grow rigid where I sat. . . . In a short period it was certain, however, that a relapse had taken place; the color disappeared from both eyelid and cheek, leaving a wanness even more than that of marble; the lips became doubly shrivelled and pinched up in the ghastly expression of death; a repulsive claminess and coldness rapidly overspread the surface of the body. . . . But why shall I minutely detail the unspeakable horrors of that night? Why shall I pause to relate how, time after time, until near the period of the gray dawn, this hideous drama of revivification was repeated; how each terrific relapse was only into a sterner and apparently more irredeemable death; how each agony wore the aspect of a struggle with some invisible foe; and how each struggle was succeeded by I know not what of wild changes in the personal appearance of the corpse?[10]

A twin horror shapes the narrator's sensations in this final section of "Ligeia," the horror of the corpse itself, of its cold and clammy flesh, a horror rehearsed, intensified with every reenactment of death, and the horror of its revivification, of a self-induced resurgence of being—a demand for life complicit with the narrator's longing, yet dangerously and appallingly alien. Even before Rowena's shroud comes undone to reveal Ligeia's distinctive features, the telltale "vehemence of desire for life," which the narrator earlier attributed to the dying Ligeia, informs the drama of revivification. Vehement desire thus betrays Ligeia's part in this drama prior to the body's actual unveiling. If from the first the narrator, like the reader, must intuit Ligeia's return, recognize in the transformations of Rowena's corpse Ligeia's indelible will to live, his intuition only accentuates the spectacle's horrific nature. In fact, it is exactly because the narrator discerns Ligeia's agency in the antics of Rowena's corpse that his own will is suspended, that the symptoms of life in the corpse produce in the teller of this tale the very symptoms of death. This relation of mutual exclusion, in which the masculine narrator cannot sustain his identity *vis-à-vis* an inflated feminine presence, is the hallmark of sentimentalism in its masculine (or elite cultural) inflection—as read and reproduced by a class of male writers who dissociate their own literary practice from that of contemporary women novelists. "Ligeia" is the narrative of sentimental motherhood told from the vantage of a rationalized masculinity, of a son whose desire for an impossible return *to* the original maternal body matches only his terror of that other possibility, that the maternal would *come (back) to him*. Inasmuch as the maternal origin figures as the site of a pre-symbolic complementarity, the fantasy of *the mother's* return, of her eruption in the symbolic, is about the loss of origins in a radically different sense—about the denaturalization of the maternal body, released from pre-history into historical time, about the irreducible contingency of the masculine subject who seeks his wholeness in the m/other. The "lost" mother's return places us beyond the fetishizing double vision of mother-as-whole, mother-as-lack; the mother cannot return as what she was (as pre-symbolic unity), and having reappeared, will no longer reduce to what she is not, to (her) lack. The mother's (re)animation "gives birth" to the very thing that the phantasm of maternal origins functions to erase— namely, the mother as historical subject.

Kaja Silverman offers a particularly compelling account of how the maternal subject disappears in/from classic psychoanalytic discourse and thus by extension, I would argue, from the bourgeois cultural imaginary: "[T]he child's discursive exteriority—its emergence from the maternal enclosure—can be established only by placing the mother herself inside that enclosure, by relegating her to the interior of [Julia Kristeva's term for this enclosure] the *chora*, or—what is the same thing—by stripping her of all linguistic capabilities."[11] Thus, Silverman suggests, the positions of the mother and of her infant are conflated. Because in the psychoanalytic account of subject formation the child's *separation from* the mother inaugurates his *relation to* the symbolic, the mother's *own* relation to language is distorted. Rather than an individuated being, herself inserted in the symbolic order, whose body assumes specific affective dimensions *for her infant,* the mother is identified with the *space* of the maternal itself, with the space of infantile dependence and verbal incapacity. In this frame, the son's yearning to return to the origin, to the "maternal enclosure," may be read less as a desire for phantasmatic connection, a recuperation of the complementarity of self and (m)other, than as an extension of the desire for autonomy. Inasmuch as the mother assumes the infant's incompetence, the son's phantasmatic return to the maternal enclosure is less a fantasy of his own regression/unmaking, than an elaboration of his mastery: the son's "return" to the maternal origin can only terminate in a recapitulation of the mother's interiorization. In the fantasy of return, the son disavows, less his own position as a differentiated subject, than his mother's. Conversely, the "lost" mother's (re)animation (re)inscribes her in history, (re)instates her as a subject in and of discourse—neither in excess of, nor (therefore) at the limit of the social. If the originary mother embodies the beyond of the social (subject), the (re)animated mother displaces this beyond, and thus opens the utopian perspective where the contingency of existing social relations becomes visible.

The utopian perspective in Poe's "Ligeia" is as fragile and elusive as the status of Rowena's body is undecidable: as a masculinist discourse, sentimentalism at once opens and forecloses on the possibility of the mother's return. On the one hand, the masculine narrator represents himself in a more or less permanent state of psychosis. The "chamber" he inhabits with Rowena and after her death is itself a Western phantasm of "oriental" luxury and decay, so that it remains finally uncertain whether the room actually exists as anything more than a projection of inner space. Likewise, Ligeia herself, as the figure whose loss this luxury both replaces and commemorates, is plausibly understood as a merely hallucinated presence in the room. On the other hand, when he reports his addiction to opium, his proneness to delusion, to the "waking visions of Ligeia" in which he indulges while sitting watch over Rowena's corpse, the narrator demonstrates a rationalist's skepticism concerning the reliability of his own senses. This conscientious acknowledgment of his impaired condition no less plausibly attests to the narrator's rationality, to his unimpeded capacity for self-evaluation, for distinguishing between "the waking vision" and the actual thing. By interrogating his own authority, the narrator underwrites the other possibility—that the sounds and motions from the bed, which have every appearance of *interrupting* his "revery," do in fact emanate from Ligeia herself.

Significantly, commentators on the tale, few in number and remarkably peremptory in their approach, bracket this carefully cultivated irresolution and subsume/subordinate Ligeia to the narrator in the most reductive and monological ways. Thus John Irwin, for instance, asserts that Ligeia is "a Psyche-figure for the narrator," a reading he derives, as far as textual evidence goes, solely from her description in the tale as a person of "gigantic volition."[12] On the contrary, Donald Pease identifies Ligeia with a primal loss, with an ineffable "something" the narrator no longer possesses: "[I]n such tales as 'Ligeia,' 'Morella,' and 'Berenice' . . . [Poe] created settings where fallen nobility could recover relation with someone or something lost."[13] The narrators of these tales "displace their present world by acting according to the demands of an archaic and infinitely more powerful past."[14] For Irwin, then, Ligeia's "gigantic volition" is identified with the masculine authorial voice, while for Pease, Ligeia's power is archaic, confined to the narrator's prelapserian past, and hence no threat to his present discursive mastery.

Ironically, while neither Pease nor Irwin read the figure of Ligeia as a mother, they assign her a mother's destiny in democracy's rationalized symbolic order; she is either invisible (a manifestation of the narrator himself), or irretrievable (belongs to the narrator's pre-history).[15] But it is this destiny, precisely, and this order, that "Ligeia" ambiguously contests *and* (re)affirms. Certainly, the narrator's reminiscences of Ligeia, and of his relation to her, insist on her pre-textual status, and so on her necessary inscription as loss. Thus the narrator's enervated diction, his obsessively refined style of portraiture—the plainly feigned naïveté with which he aspires to a mimetic perfection that the very self-consciousness of this discursive posture undermines—functions to evacuate Ligeia from the site of her re-presentation.

> In beauty of face no maiden ever equalled her. It was the radiance of an opium-dream—an airy and spirit-lifting vision more wildly divine than the phantasies which hovered about the slumbering souls of the daughters of Delos. Yet her features were not of that regular mould which we have been falsely taught to worship in the classical labors of the heathen. "There is no exquisite beauty," says Bacon, Lord Verulam, speaking truly of all the forms and *genera* of beauty, "without some strangeness in the proportion." [. . .] It might have been too that in these eyes of my beloved lay the secret to which Lord Verulam alludes. They were, I must believe, far larger than the ordinary eyes of our own race. . . . The "strangeness," however, which I found in the eyes was of a nature distinct from the formation, or the color, or the brilliancy of the features, and must, after all, be referred to the *expression*. Ah, word of no meaning! behind whose vast latitude of mere sound we intrench our ignorance of so much of the spiritual. (*LG* 176-78)

In the first moment of this portrait, Ligeia's physical beauty negates her materiality, as though perfection of form could only exist in the insubstantial medium of the vision, in the fluid dimensions of imaginary space. And while beauty in this initial moment still refers to form—Bacon's "strangeness" rests in proportions—the narrator ultimately deploys Bacon's aesthetic to locate Ligeia's beauty in what altogether exceeds her material "formation," in her "*expression*." Having transmuted Ligeia's beauty into a beauty of "*expression*," moreover, the narrator ambiguously registers the loss, abruptly empties her "*expression*" of its meaning, so that this signifier of excess, of *an excess* which still assumed at the outset a certain material specificity, becomes a cipher—the signifier of that which remains *in excess of* signification. Thus Poe, like Fuller, invests in the "expression" of a mother's face, with the fine if poignant distinction that what was in Fuller's portrait an "expression" replete with original presence becomes in Poe's a "vast latitude" of absence—an "expression" always already emptied of meaning.

But the essential significance Fuller associates with the mother attaches to Poe's Ligeia as well. As a body in excess of meaning, Ligeia becomes the repository of *all* meaning—the body of the signifiable itself:

> I have spoken of the learning of Ligeia: it was immense—such as I have never known in woman. In the classical tongues was she deeply proficient. . . . Indeed upon any theme of the most admired because simply the most abstruse of the boasted erudition of the Academy, have I *ever* found Ligeia at fault? [. . .] I said her knowledge was such as I have never known in woman—but where breathes the man who has traversed, and successfully, *all* the wide areas of moral, physical, and mathematical science? I saw not then what I now clearly perceive, that the acquisitions of Ligeia were gigantic, were astounding; yet I was sufficiently aware of her infinite supremacy to resign myself, with a child-like confidence, to her guidance through the chaotic world of metaphysical investigation at which I was most busily occupied during the earlier years of our marriage. . . . Without Ligeia I was but as a child groping benighted. (*LG* 180-81)

Ligeia is thus coextensive with the space through which this "child-like" narrator moves "benighted"; she "traverse[s]," or spans, a universe that he merely inhabits. In the frame of her "gigantic acquisitions," moreover, the figure of Ligeia herself begins to elude us, as all possible articulations of her "gigantic volition" seem *a priori* exhausted. Ligeia vanishes in the face of her own "infinite supremacy," of an unboundedness that is the negation of her subjectivity, a plenitude that leaves no room for her partiality, for her voice. Instead, it is the figure of the narrator whom we distinguish, projecting himself down the "all untrodden path" of a strangely vacant "vista":

> With how vast a triumph—with how vivid a delight—with how much of all that is ethereal in hope—did I *feel*, as she bent over me in studies but little sought—but less known—that delicious vista by slow degrees expanding before me, down whose long, gorgeous, and all untrodden path, I might at length pass onward to the goal of a wisdom too divinely precious not to be forbidden. (*LG* 180)

In this pre-symbolic realm, where learning is encoded in sensory rather than discursive registers (knowledge is felt), the figure of the mother dissolves; less a guide, or interlocutor, than an environment, she is the matrix of a masculine proto-subject—of a not-yet-subject already invested here, however, with the social and discursive primacy of the normative (white middle-class) adult male.

Inasmuch as these maternal origins inform/are informed by a masculine subjectivity elaborated at the mother's expense, the imposition of paternal law remains a narrative inevitability. The crisis of Ligeia's loss assumes conventionally oedipal dimensions: thus death acquires a phallic shape in the verses of Poe's "Conqueror Worm"—which the narrator attributes to Ligeia in Poe's revision of the tale—while the dying Ligeia's frantic invocation of the Father on hearing her poem recited confirms the bearing of paternal authority on this narrative outcome. However, to the primal horror of the phallic worm's incursion ("But see, amid the mimic rout / A crawling shape intrude! / A blood-red thing that writhes from out / The scenic solitude!"), Ligeia responds with a rage ambiguously plaintive and admonitory in quality, at once providing

and contesting the recognition of paternal ascendancy that this patriarchal God appears to exact:

> "Oh God!" half shrieked Ligeia, leaping to her feet and extending her
> arms aloft with a spasmodic movement, as I made an end to these
> lines—"Oh God! O Divine Father!—shall these things be undeviatingly
> so?—shall this conqueror be not once conquered?" (*LG* 183)

Ligeia's question is none the more answerable for being ostensibly
rhetorical in nature; inasmuch as it solicits an unequivocal response, it asks for the resolution that this narrative drama of
revivification defers. In its undecidability, Poe's "Ligeia" does not
so much unravel as simply threaten to unravel the logic of democratic representation. To replace the socially unplaced figure of
Ligeia—the narrator notes early in the tale that he never learned
her "paternal name"—he purchases a bride whose title resonates
with all the fine distinctions of social class, the "Lady Rowena
Trevanion, of Tremaine." It is to Rowena's paternally inscribed
body that Ligeia so dramatically, yet inconclusively, lays siege.

Stowe's Authentic Ghost

In the chapters of *Uncle Tom's Cabin* set on Simon Legree's plantation, Poe's drama of revivification is rescripted to accommodate
the possibility which "Ligeia" at once envisions and negates, the
possibility, that is, of the lost mother's (re)animation—as an articulate, material presence. In assigning material existence to the
spectral mother whose status Poe carefully refuses to determine,
Stowe effectively divorces presence from identity: the possibility of
the spectral mother's realization in the text hinges on the *non-
identity* of her avatars, rather than on the congruence of her mani-
festations over time. In Stowe's initial account of Legree's "pale
mother," whose silent image rises up to haunt his nights, the maternal spectre is the trace of a morality Legree suppresses, the indelible mark of maternal love on the reprobate soul. Like Poe's Ligeia,

she is ambiguously the externalization of filial dread/desire, terrifying Legree with the *promise* of a coming retribution, and a figure irreducibly other to him, whose (re)appearance *effects* his psychic/corporeal dissolution. But what follows sets Stowe's narrative apart from Poe's, and foils the normative psychoanalytic understanding of the maternal body (as a lost origin(al)) that Poe's tale at least ambiguously supports. Perceiving the effect of his mother's influence on the otherwise implacable Legree, his black slave Cassy schemes to impersonate the spectre; draping herself in white, she (re)invests the dead white mother with life. Since Stowe designates as "an authentic ghost story" this travesty of white motherhood, in this episode of the novel at least, the Good Christian Mother's authenticity comes to rest squarely on her difference from her prior incarnations. Legree's mother returns in a hybrid body, constituted in an articulation of affective motherhood and commodified reproduction. In claiming strategic possession of the white woman's spectral existence, Cassy engenders a non/white maternal subject, neither inside nor outside the order of democratic representation, but rather at the limit where this binary logic fails.

In contrast to Poe's narrator, whose terror of the mother's return is in direct proportion to his yearning for a return to the mother, Legree's distinction is his absolute lack of nostalgia for the maternal enclosure, an early and eager acquiescence in paternal law that results, paradoxically, in his repudiation of normative social forms—of the Father's (maternally mediated) message.

> Hard and reprobate as the godless man seemed now, there had been a time when he had been rocked on the bosom of a mother,—cradled with prayers and pious hymns,—his now seared brow bedewed with the waters of holy baptism. . . . Far in New England that mother had trained her only son, with long, unwearied love and patient prayers. Born of a hard-tempered sire, on whom that gentle woman had wasted a world of unvalued love, Legree had followed in the steps of his father . . . and at an early age, broke from her, to seek his fortunes at sea.[16]

What may appear by the standard of the realist novel as Stowe's flimsy characterization of Legree's innate evil points in another sense to the irrelevance of filial sentiment in the face of a structuring mythology of the masculine subject. As in Fuller's portrait, maternal love finds its expression in the pre-symbolic idiom of the essential maternal body, as it rocks and cradles the infant son. Here as well, the mother's presence reduces almost instantly to affect, operating in the service of a patriarchal authority. Legree is "cradled with prayers and pious hymns" to his heavenly Father. What distinguishes Legree from Fuller's sailor is not a respect for the paternal that leads him to follow in his earthly father's steps, but rather his failure to sentimentalize his mother's loss, to honor their affective tie. Legree is an unnatural son because he makes visible and violent the break which founds the rational subject.[17]

Legree's susceptibility to his dead mother's haunting appearance suggests the structural function of maternal love in the economy of rational subjectivity. Maternal love can be rejected as well as embraced, but never escaped. The point is that for the indifferent son, no less than for his feeling counterpart, the relation to the mother (as origin) is inescapably a relation to (the ground of) their own social subjectivity. From this perspective, the novel develops a utopian resonance at precisely the juncture where it seems most to lapse into banality:

> [Having opened a letter in which his dying mother encloses as a keepsake a lock of her golden hair] Legree burned the hair, and burned the letter; and when he saw them hissing and crackling in the flame, inly shuddered as he thought of everlasting fires. He tried to drink, and revel, and swear away the memory; but often, in the deep night, whose solemn stillness arraigns the bad soul in forced communion with herself, he had seen that pale mother rising by his bedside, and felt the soft twining of that hair around his fingers, till the cold sweat would roll down his face, and he would spring from his bed in horror. Ye who have wondered to hear, in the same evangel, that God is love, and that God is consuming fire, see ye not how, to the soul resolved in evil, perfect love is the most fearful torture, the seal and sentence of the direst despair? (*UTC* 529)

Legree cannot swear away the memory of maternal love because maternal affect mediates his relation to himself—or, in Stowe's religious teleology, to his soul. As the projection of an internal (social) limit, Legree's dead mother recalls him to himself (and to the impending consequences of his moral failing). At the same time, in the fact of the son's psychic and corporeal disarticulation, this passage registers the possibility of the mother's return: shocked past control of his body's functions, Legree breaks out in cold sweat and leaps up in inarticulate horror. His mother's appearance is ambiguously the occasion of Legree's reconstitution and decomposition as an accountable subject.

This is the scene into which Cassy inserts herself. Witness to his frenzy at the sight of little Eva's blond locks, which Legree's overseers have snatched from Tom and dutifully delivered to their master, Cassy infers the cause of Legree's terror and turns it to her own advantage. Concealing herself beneath a plain white sheet, she slips into his room by night; and when this visitation has reduced him to an impotent and inarticulate state, Cassy and her daughter substitute Emmeline, a young slave she has determined to protect from Legree's sexual advances, walk away from the plantation unmolested. Significantly, however, Cassy's affinity for the part of Legree's mother hinges for Stowe on the "influence" she already commands over Legree, an influence in turn attributed to Cassy's specifically verbal instability.

> The influence of Cassy over him was of a strange and singular kind. He was her owner, her tyrant and tormentor. . . . When he first bought her, she was, as she said, a woman delicately bred; and then he crushed her, without scruple, beneath the foot of his brutality. But, as time, and debasing influences, and despair, hardened womanhood within her, she had become in a measure his mistress, and he alternately tyrannized over and dreaded her. This influence had become more harassing and decided, since partial insanity had given *a strange, weird, unsettled cast to all her words and language*. (*UTC* 567, emphasis added)

In this section of the novel, Stowe curiously falsifies the history of Cassy's "partial insanity" as Cassy herself tells it to Uncle Tom. In Cassy's rendition, Legree is only the last in a chain of abusive masters who have "crushed her, without scruple" in pursuit of their own interests. A lovely "quadroon," born of a white father and his black concubine and raised in luxury, Cassy's first episode of abandoned rage is directed at the master who sells off her children despite her careful negotiations to prevent it, and thus finally imparts to Cassy what her history of relative privilege had kept partially from view: her displacement from the social-symbolic order as commodity, which renders any legal, emotional or conventional claim to her children unintelligible. Cassy's "unsettled" language marks her liminal relation to an order in which to speak as a black mother is to *mean* nothing at all. As though reluctant to acknowledge the connection between the black mother's grief, her painfully acquired knowledge of her own social death, and her "unsettled" language, Stowe suddenly condenses a history that elsewhere she finds useful to develop.

To trace the genesis of Cassy's "unsettled" language in the frame of this elaborated history is to reverse Stowe's emphasis in the edited account she offers us here: in this frame, Cassy's lapse from the discourse of normative femininity and Good Christian Motherhood—a discourse unavailable as a mode of self-signification to the captive African-American mother—is less the point than Cassy's capacity to *enter into* this discourse, to address Legree in the essentially maternal idiom of "influence."

> It was a cloudy, misty moonlight, and there [Legree] saw it!—something white, gliding in! He heard the still rustle of its ghostly garments. It stood still by his bed;—a cold hand touched his; a voice said, three times, in a low fearful whisper "Come! come! come!" And, while he lay sweating with terror, he knew not when or how, the thing was gone. He sprang out of bed, and pulled at the door. It was shut and locked, and the man fell down in a swoon. After this, Legree became a harder drinker than ever before. . . . There were reports around the country, soon after, that he was sick and dying. Excess had brought on that frightful disease that *seems to throw the lurid shadows of a coming retribution back into the present life.* (*UTC* 596, emphasis added)

Cassy not only performs (white) motherhood, she recodes it as a performative identity, a matter of style, of body surfaces. If in

Stowe's abolitionist polemic black mothers are just like white mothers beneath the skin, essentially the same, Cassy's performance relocates white motherhood itself in the register of imitation. On the non/white body of the white-appearing slave, white motherhood is authenticated as a likeness, a repetition rather than an originary function. Sentimentalism expires here in the shoddy trappings and crude devices of a haunting that in the very banality of its artifice abdicates a mythologized essence and reveals the utopian remainder: a deadly command to which the vanquished master submits. No longer the mother's property, "excess" transfers to the son; remarkably, it is *Cassy* who marks the *white man's* body with a condition "too frightful" to name.

Sheathed in white, Cassy's face marks the site where maternal "expression" goes blank. And while this non/white figure has no destination in Stowe's narrative, she is equally impossible to efface. Notwithstanding Stowe's desire to redomesticate Cassy, to position her in the reconstituted familial sphere to which the freed black women in this novel accede, she remains beyond Stowe's power to recall. Seeking to reinscribe Cassy's face with the tender expression of white motherhood, Stowe arranges the unlikely reunion of Cassy with her daughter, who turns out to be none other than the heroic slave mother Eliza:

> Eliza's steady, consistent piety, regulated by the constant reading of the sacred word, made her a proper guide for the shattered and wearied mind of her mother. Cassy yielded at once, and with her whole soul, to every good influence, and became a devout and tender Christian. (*UTC* 607)

Despite if not *because* of this frantic recuperation, the figure of Cassy remains in Bloch's sense "incomplete," shattered. She sits askew in these scenes of domestic resolution that conclude the novel, a "strange, unsettled" presence, marking time on a utopian calendar.

4 "Strange Coincidence"

Disavowal and History in Hawthorne and Cummins

It seems rather that when the fetish comes
to life, so to speak, some process has been
suddenly interrupted—it reminds one of the
abrupt halt made by memory in traumatic
amnesias. In the case of the fetish, too, interest
is held up at a certain point—what is possibly
the last impression received before the uncanny
traumatic one is preserved as a fetish. Thus
the foot or shoe owes its attraction as a fetish,
or part of it, to the circumstance that the
inquisitive boy used to peer up the woman's legs
toward her genitals. Velvet and fur reproduce—
as has long been suspected—the sight of the
pubic hair which ought to have revealed the
longed for penis; the underlinen so often adopted
as a fetish reproduces the scene of undressing,
the last moment at which the woman could still
be regarded as phallic.
  —Sigmund Freud, "Fetishism"

A historical materialist cannot do without the
notion of a present which is not a transition,
but in which time stands still and has come
to a stop. For this notion defines the present
in which he himself is writing history.
Historicism gives the "eternal" image of the
past; historical materialism supplies a unique
experience with the past. The historical materialist
leaves it to others to be drained by the whore
called "Once upon a time" in historicism's
bordello. He remains in control of his powers,

man enough to blast open the continuum
of history.
      —Walter Benjamin, "Theses on
      the Philosophy of History"

Like the fetishist, I too want to have it both
ways: along with psychoanalytic orthodoxy,
I will agree that female fetishism is psychically
inconceivable; while I also want to claim that
both "normal" (i.e., heterosexual) femininity
and female homosexuality can be seen in socio-
political terms in excess of their psychoanalytic
descriptions, as modes of fetishism (in the same
way that, I would claim, feminism can be seen
as a form of mass or collective psychosis, a
political disavowal of women's social reality
as oppressed).
      —Elizabeth Grosz, "Lesbian Fetishism?"

What is the fetishist's relation to history, conceived as heterogeneous time? In other words, following Walter Benjamin, the
fetishist's relation to a *contested* history, engendered in the present,
as a rupture in the coherence of the past? Both Benjamin's historical materialist and Freud's fetishist are figures arrested in time,
brought up short before the contemplation of a discontinuity, a
rift in (the body of) the past. However, in Freud's account, the
fetishist disavows the lack which the discovery of sexual difference has blasted in the continuum of his pre-oedipal history. His
arrest only affirms the coherence of what precedes it, preserves
the "Once upon a time" of maternal integrity in the form of the
fetish object. As such, Freud's fetishist has more in common with
Benjamin's unmanned "others" and their linear or cumulative con-

ception of history, in which the past is the already given, a fixed or "'eternal' image."

For both Freud's fetishist and Benjamin's naive historicist, the past is a phantasmatic *space,* on the boundary of time; time becomes the dimension of a "transitional" present, always incomplete with respect to its antecedent. In contrast, Benjamin's historical materialist unambiguously affirms the discontinuity or difference in and of the past. Where Freud's fetishist insists on the integrity of his past despite its newly apparent heterogeneity, the historical materialist seizes on and magnifies the heterogeneity of the past to defeat the image of historical coherence that underwrites as a given the existing relations of power. Thus the historical materialist manfully cracks open the body of the past and conceives/constructs history as a temporality of transformation. From this perspective, Benjamin's phallic materialist displays an unexpected political affinity with Elizabeth Grosz's delusional feminists. Unlike Freud's fetishist, who comes to a halt before the reality of paternal law, Grosz's female fetishist/feminist appears instead to enter into juridical and political time in order to subvert it from within. As we move from Freud to Grosz, fetishism exceeds its psychoanalytic description as a state of psychic arrest, to become a "mode" of being in the world, a logic or style of political dissent. Like the historical materialist, Grosz's feminist fetishist values the past, presumably not for its integrity, but for its disjunctures or seams, from which she disengages alternatives to the established social reality. I argue, then, that we can situate Freud, Benjamin, and Grosz as the three moments of a dialectic: Freud's notion of fetishism as a form of ahistorical resistance to paternal law finds its negation in Benjamin's construction of historical resistance as the phallic violation of an eternalized and feminized past; and Freud and Benjamin find their synthesis in Grosz's reinvention of fetishism as a historically situated modality of feminist resistance.

I invoke Benjamin in order to specify how a feminist reclaiming of disavowal as a modality of resistance requires not only (in strictly psychoanalytic terms) a feminization of fetishism, but also (insofar as we can agree that feminism is the practice of an oppositional historical consciousness) a revision of the fetishist's relation to the temporality of history, which Freud's fetishist craftily concedes to the father, so as to preserve the maternal phallus intact, beyond the transformative operations of historical time. Benjamin's critique of bourgeois historicism for its eternalizing of the past thus suggests why masculine fetishism is not an oppositional practice at all; fetishism shares its fundamentally ahistorical and idealist impulse with a bourgeois historicism that fixes the past as the ground (or necessity) of the present order. But Benjamin's telling metaphoric construction of history's "continuum" as a feminized body only functions to open this body to violent penetration by the masculine materialist mind. In this context, I conclude that a feminist mode of disavowal must somehow double as a critique and a disruption of this very linkage of the feminine body to a spatialized (continuous) past.[1] How does Grosz think a notion of fetishism that functions precisely to reclaim transformative history for women, to resituate the fetishized maternal body in relation to paternal time and the established symbolic order?

I need to emphasize that the question as I have posed it here is not exactly the one Grosz poses to herself in "Lesbian Fetishism?" In fact, Grosz's construction of feminism as collective disavowal remains parenthetical to her argument. Nonetheless, I contend that her model of lesbian fetishism alters the terms of freudian fetishism to accommodate the notion of feminist disavowal and/or feminism as disavowal, and more particularly that her rescripting of Freud involves her reconceptualization of the mother's relation to history. In the first section of this chapter, I want to trace the passage from a freudian to a feminist fetishism. In the second and third sections, however, I complicate the dialectical progression— from fetishism, through historical materialism to feminist fetishism—I outlined earlier, by locating these two types of fetishism in two more or less contemporaneous texts, Nathaniel

Hawthorne's *The Blithedale Romance* (1852) and Maria Susanna Cummins's *The Lamplighter* (1854). Ultimately, then, while renegotiating the meaning of Cummins's literary practice *via* Grosz, I displace Grosz *via* Cummins from the historical movement in which I began by situating her, to produce a nonlinear history of these women's oppositional discourses.

The Signification of the Maternal Phallus

The mark of the fetishist is his duplicitous response to maternal castration, which he simultaneously knows and refuses to know. Exactly what is lost in the knowledge of maternal castration—what two moments or modalities of the child's existence lie on either side of this great divide? Freud's account of how the normative little boy accedes to knowledge of the mother's lack is interestingly unstable, particularly with respect to the mother's status before the paternal interdiction of her body is in force. While seeking to situate the maternal body as both prior and subject to patriarchal law, Freud borders on exposing the mother's historicity, as a subject at once internal and potentially resistant to it. I want to consider the bearing of this latter construction of the maternal on the signification of the maternal phallus, and by extension, its bearing on the politics of fetishism.

In "The Splitting of the Ego," Freud specifies that the spectacle of the woman's genitals alone is insufficient to compel belief in maternal castration. (Initially, that is, the child resists the spectacularization of the female body, as the locus of sexual difference.) Likewise, the articulation of the paternal threat produces no "great impression" by itself. Only when ocular proof is conjoined to paternal law does the child embrace, as Freud puts it elsewhere, "the reality of the threat that he had hitherto laughed at."[2]

A threat of castration by itself need not produce a great impression. The child will refuse to believe in it, for he cannot easily imagine the possibility of losing such a highly prized part of his body. A sight of the female genitals, on the other hand, might convince him of that possibility. But he would draw no conclusion from this alone, since his disinclination to doing so would be too great and *there would be no motive present which would compel him to*. [. . .] But it is different if both factors are present together. In that case the threat revives the memory of the perception, which had hitherto been regarded as harmless.[3] (Emphasis added)

What is the meaning of the interval between the child's perception of women's castration and his acknowledgment of its "truth"—between his first sight of the female genitals (where this precedes the castration threat) and the advent of his capacity to see—that is, in this instance, to see what is *not* there? As Freud would have it, the little boy is *a priori* averse to recognizing the absence in women of such a "highly prized part" of himself and accedes to the truth only under duress, where verbal threat and visual display converge and bear witness to each other. In this scenario, the father's castration threat compels an irresistible association of ideas, in which women's lack now appears to place the boy-child's own organ in danger. We might interpret castration, then, to mean the following: the little boy is induced to concede that the mother lacks the phallus, so that he may receive it from the father.

In this zone between perception and avowal, we encounter the little boy *on the verge* of his initiation into the economy of sexual difference: although already confronted with women's lack, the perception causes such distress that he reflexively screens it, and must be made to see through his own devices, against "the force of the opposite wish."[4] Paradoxically, then, the maternal phallus is designed to *fend off* knowledge of women's difference—paradoxically, because the little boy here wields the very mark of difference to affirm his identity in and with the maternal body. Ruth Mack Brunswick offers the most cogent rendering of this scenario:

[The belief in the maternal phallus functions] to insure the mother's possession of the penis, and as such probably *arises at the moment when the child becomes uncertain that the mother does indeed possess it.* Previously [. . .] it seems more than probable that the executive organ of the

active mother is the breast; the idea of the penis is then *projected back*
upon the active mother after the importance of the phallus has been
recognised. (Emphasis added)[5]

The little boy's belief in the maternal phallus thus would function
as a plaster on the newly discovered insufficiency of the pre-
oedipal maternal body. By covering over the missing piece, he
seeks to suspend the mother's mutation from a giver-of-the-breast
in a pre-phallic (dyadic) economy into the figure of lack within the
triadic economy of paternal law. In brief, every mother's son starts
out a fetishist, salvaging the all-in-all of the maternal body even
before he *knows* it to be lost. Unlike the fetishist's, the little boy's
visceral or immediate disavowal is a tenuous and futile gesture,
precisely because it remains prior to the imposition of the law, to
the child's induction in the patriarchal order; by contrast, Freud's
fetishist has undergone the trauma of "both factors" (both the sight
of women's mutilated genitals and the articulation of the paternal
threat). Thus he bends to the law, displacing the imaginary organ
from the maternal body, preserving it in the elsewhere of the fetish
object. But I remark the phenomenon of the little boy's visceral disavowal for what it suggests about the signification of the maternal
phallus, which Freud erects as a bulwark against the disruption of
the dyadic. Consequently, the belief in the maternal phallus is
necessarily in conflict with any reality we can "erect," because it is
a belief in the "once upon a time" of complementarity with the
mother, in the sufficiency of a pre-phallic, pre-discursive economy.

Still, Freud leaves the door ajar to another reading, in which we
recast the interplay of knowledge and belief, and fetishism
emerges in a different relation to discourse. The lag between perception and avowal harbors something resistant to Freud's conclusions. For Freud, the little boy's *apparent* (initial) *indifference* to
the sight of the female genitals is, above all, not *really* indifference,
but an index of a primary anxiety—primary, in the sense that it is
posited, not derived. It remains axiomatic in Freud's analysis that
the existence of bodies unlike the child's own, with respect to

sexual anatomy at least, is a source of vexation and distress. Nevertheless, it is always possible to imagine that the little boy's quaint conclusions about female anatomy—the little girl will grow a penis later, he typically declares—represent no more nor less than what they seem: a rather cursory engagement with the "problem" of the missing penis. Moreover, if the little boy has initially no particular stake in the configurations of the female body, it is arguably that the mother remains in any case visibly in possession of that which is *valued*—of the phallus and of the *authority* it confers. This reading against the grain of Freud's analysis, a reading which, I want to suggest, nevertheless shadows Freud's text, implicitly shifts us away from a freudian to a lacanian frame of reference, in which the phallus is understood, not as the extension of the penis, but as the mark or trace of its absence. As Elizabeth Grosz puts it,

> . . . the penis (as real organ) can only take on the role of the phallus because it is *missing*, i.e., because women are castrated [. . .] From being a real organ, the penis is transformed into an imaginary object, dividing the sexes according to its presence or absence, possessed by some and desired by others. Only then can it function as a symbolic object (an object of union/exchange) between the sexes. The phallus distributes access to the social categories invested with various power relations. . . .[6]

While in Freud's narrative the little boy is naturally disinclined to remark the absence in the woman of his own most "highly prized part," a part he prizes for the satisfaction or masturbatory pleasure it affords him, for Lacan the registers of satisfaction and desire remain absolutely distinct; it is only in consequence of its absence in the woman that the phallus becomes properly speaking the "prize," and hence a thing one might nonetheless wish to attribute to particular women. From this perspective, the little boy's belief in the maternal phallus cannot precede or defer his knowledge of sexual difference, since that knowledge underwrites the "transformation" or elevation of the anatomical penis into the symbolic phallus—although this belief plainly does defer recognition of *how the phallus circulates* within the economy of patriarchal gender. Simply stated, the belief in the maternal phallus can hardly function to preserve a properly pre-phallic or dyadic relation to the maternal body, when the phallus *is* the third term, the dimension of the symbolic itself, of intersubjective relations.

Indeed, for Lacan, what we might designate with various emphases the pre-symbolic, dyadic, or object relation to the mother ("object" because this relation "conjoins to the need an object that satisfies it") is the vanishing point of the analytic gaze.

> [W]e must start off with a radical intersubjectivity, with the subject's total acceptance by the other subject. It is by starting with the experience of the adult that me must grapple retrospectively, *nachträglich,* with the supposedly original experiences, in ranging the various degradation in tiers, without ever leaving the domain of intersubjectivity. Insofar as we remain within the register of analysis, we will be obliged to admit an original intersubjectivity.
>
> There is no transition possible between the two registers, between that of animal desire, in which the relation is object, and that of the recognition of desire. There has to be intersubjectivity at the beginning, since it is there at the end.[7]

Lacan posits an "original intersubjectivity" because there is simply no way to *derive* intersubjectivity from the mother/child relation conceived as a relation of "complementarity," symbiosis or sufficiency. The latter is located in the register of "animal desire," of the desire for the satisfaction of needs, a desire that knows fulfillment because the "subject" of desire in this case does not see himself desiring. Intersubjectivity, however, engages the register of "the recognition of desire," or, as Lacan puts its elsewhere, of the *demand* for satisfaction that is always excessive with respect to anything that satisfies a need.[8]

> There is never a simple duplicity of terms. It is not only that I see the other. I see him seeing me, which implicates the third term, namely that he knows that I see him. The circle is closed. There are always three terms in the structure, even if these three terms are not explicitly present.[9]

The Other mediates the subject's recognition of desire (the Other sees me seeing him) and insofar as there is an Other (a duplicity of terms), there is recognition of desire (a triadic or intersubjective relation).

In Grosz's revision of Freud, I remark a subtle but crucial (re)deployment of the potentially radical and denaturalizing implications of Lacan's argument. It is, of course, with this denaturalization of sexual and familial relations that the most persuasive among Lacan's feminist promoters have credited him.[10] However, Lacan's own displacement of the mother/child relation into the domain of intersubjectivity, of the symbolic and of history, is conspicuously abortive. That is, the work of de-naturalization is arrested, precisely at the juncture where it entails summoning the mother forward into history: somewhere in the passage from an object relation to an "original intersubjectivity," the mother herself is erased, transmuted into a masculine pronoun ("I see *him* seeing me . . "). Having posited the concept of "original intersubjectivity," Lacan's critique of the object relation shifts rhetorical and conceptual gears, and we find ourselves progressing through a quasi-sartrian dialectic of being and otherness, marked by the peculiar *Aufhebung* of the m/other into a "him." Thus it becomes crucial to distinguish between Lacan's rescripting of Freud, and Grosz's rescripting of Freud *via* Lacan.

As Grosz deploys the lacanian phallus, the little boy's attribution of the phallus to the mother no longer qualifies, *a priori* at least, as a gesture any more or less delusional (any more or less in conflict with a *possible,* if not an actual, reality) than his attribution of the phallus to the father. By investing the mother with the phallus, the little boy pays tribute, not to her integrity, but to her position of authority within an economy of symbolic exchange. Grosz puts it this way:

> The fetish is a substitute for, a talisman of, the phallus, but not just any old phallus. For the pre-oedipal boy, the most valued of phalluses is not his own (for his pre-oedipal, imaginary penis is not yet elevated to the

function of phallus) but his mother's—the phallus, that is, *that endows her with power and authority.* (Incidentally, it is precisely her role and function as phallic mother that covers over and hides her status as a woman, her sexual difference from the son.) He must disavow maternal castration if he is to protect himself from his own castration. (*LF* 42-43, emphasis added)

Implicit in this passage, and particularly in its parentheses, is the status of the pre-oedipal mother as subject. We are situated here prior to the paternal interdiction of the mother (prior to the little boy's accession to gendered subjectivity, to his identification with the father and the elevation of his imaginary penis "to the function of the phallus"),[11] but *not* prior to (sexual) difference and/as his recognition of positions or "categories invested with various power relations." From this vantage (or in this register), the maternal phallus occludes, not the inadequacy of the maternal body, but the mother's social and symbolic status as a woman. Furthermore, this construction of the maternal phallus suggests an alternative conception of oedipal socialization—of what may be said to occur when the little boy accepts his mother's castration (and so too the possibility of his own) and submits to paternal law. For Freud, castration means that the little boy reluctantly comes to know women's lack and identifies with the father as the figure of phallic authority. Grosz's formulation implies instead that what the normative son must concede is his mother's *femininity* (where femininity is the destined position of the sexed female body in the social-symbolic order) and the resulting redistribution of phallic authority, henceforth to be sought exclusively through the father. In the second scenario, the mother's lack is less a "truth" avowed in consequence of the father's castration threat, than an effect of paternal law itself.[12]

The revisions which Grosz effects on the freudian model of the (male) fetishist are determining for her model of lesbian fetishism, since for the lesbian fetishist, the refusal of castration turns on the displacement of "phallic value" to another *subject.* Grosz begins by remarking the similarity between the trajectory of the male fetishist and that of the "masculine woman" as Freud describes them:

> In the path that produces the masculinity complex, there is a disavowal of women's castration and a refusal to acknowledge the socially sanctioned meaning of sexual difference. The girl will continue to identify with the phallic mother, and may even see the father as simply another embodiment of the phallic status of the mother (it is significant that this is the fate of the male fetishist as well). In refusing to acknowledge her difference from the phallic position, she retains the masculinity of her pre-oedipal position and the mother as love-object. (LF 51)

Furthermore, unlike either the hysteric or the narcissist, who "phallicize or fetishize their own bodies," the masculine woman reproduces "the fetishistic structure of the displacement of the phallus from the mother's body to an object outside oneself." Here, however, the masculine and the lesbian fetishists part company.

> [The masculine woman] displaces phallic value onto an object outside the mother's (or her own) phallus; but in contrast to the fetishist, her love-object is not an inanimate or partial object, but rather another subject. Her "fetish" is not the result of a fear of femininity, but a love of it; it does not protect her from potential danger, for it introduces her to the effects of widespread social homophobia. (LF 51)

Rather than conserve the maternal phallus in the elsewhere of the fetish, in an object wrenched from the transformative time of history, the lesbian fetishist conserves the pre-oedipal distribution of phallic authority in the actuality of her sexual relations and her domestic arrangements. That is, she at once identifies with the phallic mother and so retains possession of the phallus (disavows her own castration), and she displaces the phallus as signifier of the mother's value onto another female subject (desires women). Consequently, while the male fetishist enjoys the fetish object privately, at the level of imaginary identifications not readily deciphered or penetrated by the public gaze (the fetish object is a kind of solipsism, whose value, as Freud observes, is known only to the fetishist), the lesbian fetishist "erects" the maternal phallus both at the level of imaginary identifications and of intersubjective relations—which places her, as Grosz underscores, in conflict with an established heterosexist social order, and subject to its retributions.

Rereading Freud's paradigmatic male fetishist through the lens of "Lesbian Fetishism?," it becomes possible to distinguish two forms or modalities of fetishism, corresponding to two ways of apprehending the maternal phallus. In the first modality, which I call masculine fetishism, the maternal phallus stands as the monument to a lost complementarity with the mother, and its value is conserved (its loss disavowed) in the space of the fetish object. Whatever we might want to claim about the actual (the historical) configuration of the masculine fetishist's pre-oedipal relation to the mother, the fantasy invested in the fetish object is one of maternal sufficiency.[13] Typically, this fetishist is "quite content" with the "advantages . . . for erotic gratification" of his love-object, and indeed, Freud reminds us, gratification by means of the fetish object is "very convenient," because "[t]he fetishist has no trouble in getting what other men have to woo and exert themselves to obtain."[14] Indeed, from this perspective, we might consider classing fetishism as a kind of object relation, in which the fetishist "conjoins" to desire an object to which he has assigned the property of satisfying desire. (Of course, the point is not that, for the fetishist, desire terminates in satisfaction, but that the pursuit of satisfaction *in the object* evokes a phantasmatic maternal economy of sufficiency.) In the second modality, which I designate feminist fetishism, the maternal phallus is the signifier of the mother's social-symbolic authority, and its value is invested in a female subject. The fetish here evokes the possibility of extra-patriarchal intersubjectivity; in other words, the possibility of investing subjects with authority in excess of and in opposition to the distribution of authority within the economy of patriarchal gender.

For Grosz, it is the practice of disavowal "which inclines [the lesbian fetishist] to feminism, insofar as feminism, like any oppositional movement, involves a disavowal of social reality so that change becomes conceivable and possible" (*LF* 51). In this section, I have sought to elucidate how the content of the loss that the fetishist disavows bears on the politics of his or her disavowal, with reference specifically to the historical location (pre-symbolic or symbolic) of the oppositional fantasy to which the fetishist subscribes. Whereas the masculine fetishist remains, as Freud suggests, a figure arrested in time, whose contestation of the status quo turns on the preservation and the private enjoyment of a phantasmatic pre-history, the feminist fetishist preserves the possibility of a female subject's emancipation from patriarchal gender. She installs her fantasy at the level of her social-symbolic practice, particularly in and by a reconfiguration of domestic space. As such, her practice involves the alignment of her present with the *difference* in and of her past, and moves, at least potentially, toward the production of alternative futures.

Masculine Fetishism and Narrative Temporalities

The narrator of Nathaniel Hawthorne's *The Blithedale Romance* exemplifies the investment of the masculine fetishist in a fantasy of the mother's body as a site of pre-symbolic complementarity. At the same time, the narrator attempts to activate or install his fetish in the mode of the feminist fetishist—that is, to "erect" it in a nontraditional domestic order, in and as the utopian familial/communal space of Blithedale. As Miles Coverdale tells it, the failure of this agrarian socialist collective (modelled on the Brook Farm community where Hawthorne spent just over six months in 1841) points less to the limits of agrarian socialism than to the limits of masculine fetishism as a social and political practice. Coverdale's narration, that is, discloses the paradoxical way in which the fetishist's desire for the archaic maternal body disavows the condition of its own possibility; the masculine fetishist recurs obsessively to the impasse inherent in desire itself, that makes desire incommensurate with any object said to satisfy it. Rather than engender a space where "change becomes conceivable," where alternative configurations of intersubjectivity emerge (in the mode of Grosz's feminist fetishist, who disavows the determinations of feminine gender in patriarchy), Coverdale turns in an imaginary circuit around the division in the (desiring) subject.

If Freud's paradigmatic fetishist is an exceptionally happy subject, basking in the free access to his "conveniently" situated object, we can distinguish Hawthorne's Coverdale by his disenchantment with his own desire, and his ultimate recognition of his own incapacity for agency, history, narrative itself. *Blithedale* begins with Coverdale's removal to the prelapsarian economy of Blithedale farm (where "blitheness" fills out the "dale" or rift in the subject produced by his accession to the order of the "cover" or the signifier?) and the pre-oedipal economy of Zenobia's body (it is worth recalling that the historical Zenobia ruled Palmyra in the name of her infant son), only to terminate in his arrest—in his coming-to-a-halt before the figure of Zenobia's veiled double, Priscilla. While Coverdale imagines himself in movement toward the integral maternal body, the novel's ending reveals him frozen in the posture of masculine disavowal: a fascinated spectator before the veiled female form. *Blithedale* thus returns Coverdale to his point of origin as speaking subject; the narrator's restoration of the phallic maternal body in the marginal spaces of Blithedale farm, his disavowal of maternal lack, results in disavowal, in a reiteration of belief against the force of a *still incontrovertible knowledge*. Such a conclusion implies, not so much that Coverdale's path is circular, as that his position is fixed at the outset, that his ostensible displacements (to Blithedale farm; back again to a metropolitan scene) are somehow counterfeit, inscribed in the text but not authorized by the logic of the fetishist's desire. In other words, Coverdale's narrative suggests how fetishism is resistant to narrative temporalities; fetishism marks the masculine subject's refusal of his historical dislocations, starting of course with his originary dislocation, from the site of an imputed maternal origin into historical time.

Coverdale's narrative "unfolds," then, something like this: Fixated on Zenobia, whose "luxurious" body fills his visual and psychic horizon, Coverdale expends his energies piecing together her history out of rumor, innuendo, and tantalizing fragments of conversations only half overheard. Known to the "public" as a woman of means, a noted writer and campaigner for women's rights, Zenobia was once bound (perhaps in marriage) to the mesmerist Professor Westervelt, whom she escapes at the implied cost of enslaving to him her half-sister, Priscilla. Westervelt demonstrates his mesmerical powers at town-hall "lectures," where he exhibits Priscilla as the enigmatic "Veiled Lady" and dispatches her, before enthusiastic crowds, to the elsewhere of the "spirit world." Meanwhile, released from the Veil and her ties to Westervelt, Zenobia comes before the world, the undiminished original of womanhood, emitting an

> influence . . . such as we might suppose to come from Eve, when she was just made, and her creator brought her to Adam, saying—"Behold, here is a woman." Not that [Coverdale] would convey the idea of especial gentleness, grace, modesty and shyness, but of a certain warm and rich characteristic, which seems, for the most part, to have been refined away out of the feminine system.[15]

Soon after Coverdale's arrival at Blithedale, however, Priscilla appears as well, in flight from the fraudulent hypnotist, to implore Zenobia's protection. Coverdale gazes in disbelief at the shrinking, pallid, "unsubstantial" form of Zenobia's sibling, a woman incapable, "in her densest moments, [of] mak[ing] herself quite visible," and so only really visible when veiled (*BR* 187). Yet Coverdale's incredulity notwithstanding, in the course of the narrative, every character (not excepting Priscilla herself) mysteriously transfers his or her investment from Zenobia to Priscilla, who is finally liberated from the magician's clutches into the "veiled happiness" of marriage with the ineffectual social reformer Hollingsworth (*BR* 242). Her own passion for Hollingsworth thus thwarted and her fortune mysteriously lost (how and by whom we never learn), Zenobia declares to Coverdale her intention to assume the nun's "black-veil," but drowns herself that very night

in the river's black waters. Angry and bereft in the wake of Zenobia's suicide, Coverdale leaves Blithedale for good, to resume his
former, phlegmatic existence in the city. But he startles the reader
on the novel's much commented-on last page with a confession of
love for Hollingsworth's veiled bride.

Despite Coverdale's assertion that "the confession, brief as it shall
be, will throw a gleam of light over my behavior throughout the
foregoing incidents" (BR 247), nothing in the text invites the reader
to anticipate Coverdale's disclosure. Among *Blithedale*'s critics,
Richard Brodhead queries the point of this ending most emphatically, asserting that it retroactively imposes on the reader a plainly
untenable interpretation of events. If "Coverdale's confession is
true, then nothing else in the novel" can be, Brodhead complains,
and the reader is finally "stranded in a series of surrealistic per-
spectives."[16] However, Coverdale's assertion that it was Priscilla he
desired all along "strand[s]" us only insofar as we assume that
his object of desire is a woman, a particular female subject. If we
recognize instead that Coverdale's investment is in the veil, in
the fetish that (re)covers both women's lack, it matters relatively
little which of the two sisters Coverdale professes to adore.
Although there is an important slippage in the trajectory of
Coverdale's desire for which we must account, it is with respect to
the narrator's *choice of fetish,* I would argue, rather than his choice
of woman. While his relation to Zenobia is marked by Coverdale's
fetishizing of representation (so that, we might say, *The Blithedale
Romance* is his fetish object), his relation to Priscilla at the novel's
end is marked by his fetishizing of silence—of that which disrupts
and discontinues representation.

More particularly, Coverdale's representations of Zenobia constitute the veil over the absence that his capacity for discourse
necessarily invokes in the archaic maternal body. Zenobia's name
is a pseudonym, that dissembles the identity of its bearer, Coverdale acknowledges, "a sort of mask in which she comes before the
world, retaining all the privileges of privacy—a contrivance, in
short, *like the white drapery of the Veiled Lady,* only a little more

transparent" (*BR* 8, emphasis added), so that to name Zenobia is by definition to cover her over. From this perspective, "Zenobia" stands in relation to Priscilla, not as the original to the copy, as "womanliness incarnated" to her incorporeal half-sister, but as one Veiled Lady to another. At the same time, "Zenobia" functions precisely to occlude the loss of origins, to transform the female body into a phantasmatic space, where the division in the desiring subject is made good.

> Her hand, though very soft, was larger than most women would like to have—or than they could afford to have—though not a whit too large *in proportion with the spacious plan of Zenobia's development.* (*BR* 15, emphasis added)

Pursuing these architectural metaphors, Coverdale describes Zenobia's "*mellow, almost broad laugh*—most delectable to hear, but not in the least like an ordinary women's laugh" (*BR* 16, emphasis added). Moreover, "the world never criticize[s] her so harshly as it does most women who transcend its rules," he asserts, because "the sphere of ordinary womanhood was *felt to be narrower than her development required*" (*BR* 190, emphasis added). By figuring "Zenobia" as a space, rather than as a subject bounded by, or located in, time and space, Coverdale restructures the dialectics of the gaze:

> [Zenobia] should have made it a point of duty, moreover, to sit endlessly to painters and sculptors, and preferably to the latter; because the cold decorum of the marble would consist with the utmost scantiness of drapery, so the eye might chastely be gladdened with her material perfection, in its entireness. I know not well how to express, that the native glow of colouring of her cheeks, and even the flesh-warmth of the round arms, and what was visible of her full bust—in a word, her womanliness incarnated—compelled me sometimes to close my eyes, as if it were not quite the privilege of modesty to gaze at her. (*BR* 44)

Rather than perceive her from a differentiated subject position, Coverdale appears to look on Zenobia from within her "sphere,"

from within the charmed circle of her "glow" or "flesh-warmth."
He inhabits both the position of desiring subject *and* of the object
of his gaze, becomes at once viewer and viewed. This continuity
is legible in Coverdale's peculiar capitulation to "modesty," for it
is after all not *Coverdale's* modesty, but *Zenobia's*, whose "privilege"
is violated by his prurient gaze. The sudden eruption of the
object's shame in the discourse of the viewing subject affirms
Coverdale's impossible position *within* the space of the other on
whom he looks. In Coverdale's phantasmatic scripting of Zenobia's body, then, we exit the domain of intersubjectivity: having
colonized both positions, Coverdale can neither see Zenobia
seeing him, or know that she knows him to be seeing her.

But this fantasy of complementarity inaugurates Coverdale's
reinsertion into the symbolic order in the later portions of the
novel. Increasingly dominated by Hollingsworth, who commands
the women's devotion but alienates Coverdale with his plans to
transform Blithedale into a post-lapsarian community, given over
to the reformation of criminals, Blithedale becomes the scene of
crisis from which Coverdale takes flight:

> I was beginning to lose the sense of what kind of world it was, among
> innumerable schemes of what it might be or ought to be. It was impos-
> sible, situated as we were [at Blithedale], not to imbibe the idea that
> everything in nature was fluid, or fast becoming so; so that the crust of
> the earth, in many places, was broken, and its whole surface porten-
> tously upheaving; that it was a day of crisis. . . . (*BR* 140)

Under the pressure of Hollingsworth's scheme, Blithedale begins
to distinguish itself most markedly from the world beyond it, as
fluidity from "the settled system of things," suggesting the retrospective construction of the pre-oedipal that Judith Roof succinctly
remarks. "The celebrated preoedipal lack of differentiation is actually a perceptual product of differentiation";[17] thus we see
Blithedale assume its most distinctly pre-oedipal character at
precisely the moment when Coverdale begins to (re)emerge into

intersubjectivity. His flight from the fluid topographies of Blithedale marks his entry into the mirror stage, which, as Roof sum-
marizes, "not only presages a concept of separate self . . . [but] also
initiates the child into history." Paying a visit to Zenobia's city
dwelling, Coverdale finds himself amidst

> [p]ictures, marbles, vases; in brief, more shapes of luxury than there
> could be any object in enumerating, except for an auctioneer's adver-
> tisement—and the whole repeated and doubled by the reflection of a
> great mirror, which showed me Zenobia's proud figure, likewise, and my
> own. It cost me, I acknowledge, a bitter sense of shame, to perceive in
> myself a positive effort to bear up against the effect which Zenobia
> sought to impose on me. (BR 164)

The mirror stage projects Coverdale, in anticipatory fashion, into
the symbolic, where the pre-oedipal maternal body now appears
as *too* large and affecting, as a body in excess, so that Coverdale
takes care to decipher the inscription of the mother's imminent
impoverishment, in the form of the auctioneer's advertisement, an-
nouncing, presumably, the sale of her worldly possessions.

Thus Coverdale's removal to Blithedale and his imaginary retrogression toward the undifferentiated maternal body only return
him to the threshold of the symbolic, where the mother is simultaneously visible in her newly apparent excess and prospectively
inscribed as lacking, divested of her "imaginary opulence" (BR 216).
But having acknowledged a magnification of the maternal which
only announces its eclipse, Coverdale promptly disavows the
mother's destiny: "But, the next instant, she was too powerful for all
my opposing struggles. I saw how fit it was that she should make
herself as gorgeous as she pleased, and should do a thousand things
that would have been ridiculous in the poor, thin, weakly characters of other women" (BR 165). From this vantage, however, we can
identify "the poor, thin, weakly" Priscilla as Zenobia's mirror image
in both senses of the term, as her (incorporeal) inverse, of course,
but also as her inscription. Priscilla is the depredation of the
auctioneer writ large: "There was a lack of human substance in her;

it seemed as if, were she to stand up in a sunbeam, it would pass right through her figure, and trace out the cracked and dusty window-panes upon the naked floor" (*BR* 185). Unlike Zenobia, then, Priscilla *is* her name.

> Priscilla! Priscilla! I repeated the name to myself, three or four times; and, in that little space, this quaint and prim cognomen had so amalgamated itself with my idea of the girl, that it seemed as if no other name could have adhered to her for a moment. (*BR* 29)

While "Zenobia" is a discursive veil over a body imagined to precede its naming, "Priscilla" is the inscription of a dispossessed femininity that must be veiled if we are to believe in her embodiment. Coverdale's imaginary retrogression toward Zenobia's originary maternal body (re)turns him at the novel's end to "Priscilla," to the horizon where "Zenobia" vanishes. However, Coverdale's (latest) recognition of the loss of origins provokes rather than precludes his disavowal of the mother's lack: thus he averts his gaze from the insubstantial Priscilla, on the novel's final page, in a gesture of *feminine* modesty that signals his phantasmatic return to the place of the (m)other.

> The reader, therefore, since I have disclosed so much, is entitled to this one word more. As I write it, he will charitably suppose me to blush, and turn away my face:—I—I myself—was in love—with—PRISCILLA! (*BR* 247)

Once again, then, we witness the eruption of the object's shame in the viewing subject (although the identification of subject and object that we are "charitably" to "suppose" is here partially undermined by the syntax of the final line, which drives manfully forward from subject to verb to object). Coverdale's expression of blushing embarrassment thus announces what the final line displays: that he has (re)invested the dispossessed female body with "Zenobia's" surplus, or, in other words, has capitalized Priscilla. But where *Blithedale*'s narrator began by fetishizing rep-

resentation itself, his confession of love for "PRISCILLA" speaks
to a de-fetishizing of representation at the novel's close: as we
move from "Zenobia" to "PRISCILLA," the woman's name
becomes the signifier of loss, the thing to be veiled. Masculine
fetishism finally emerges as incommensurate with narrative, when
the narrator recognizes as his proper fetish that which discontinues representation, the pauses (visually rendered in the dash) that
suspend our approach to "PRISCILLA" and graphically disarticulate the text of his confession.

Blithedale thus leaves Coverdale arrested (anew) before the loss
of the archaic maternal body and the division in the desiring subject. At the same, the novel gestures, if only tentatively, toward an
alternative conception of the maternal—toward a conception of
non-original maternity. On the one hand, as I have argued here, in
his representations of "Zenobia," Coverdale disavows the loss of
complementarity implicit in his very capacity to represent the
mother, so that "Zenobia's" counterfeit presence emits, paradoxically, the aura of authenticity in which it is "the grown-up men
and women" of Blithedale who appear as mere masqueraders.

> [T]he presence of Zenobia caused our heroic enterprise to show like an
> illusion, a masquerade, a pastoral, a counterfeit Arcadia, in which we
> grown-up men and women were making a plaything of the years that
> were given us to live in. (*BR* 21)

Toward the novel's end, however, the possibility (briefly) surfaces
that the mother's value might inhabit the symbolic—that "Zenobia's" corporeality is not atemporal and pre-discursive, but historical and stylized. Taking part in a communal masquerade,
"Zenobia" *assumes* the role of "Queen Zenobia," as if finally, and
shortly before her death, allowed to come into her own as *subject*.

> She represented the Oriental princess, by whose name we were accus-
> tomed to know her. Her attitude was free and noble, yet, if a queen's, it
> was not that of a queen triumphant, but dethroned, on trial for her life,

or perchance condemned already. The spirit of conflict seemed, nevertheless, to be alive in her. (*BR* 213)

About to be deposed, "Zenobia" appropriates her own mask in a kind of second degree masquerade—masquerades as being her name/mask, and thereby makes "Zenobia" over as a contested zone. Significantly, Zenobia's downfall is rendered here in the metaphor of "dethroning" or deposition, rather than of dispossession: at issue is the loss or displacement of (maternal) authority, rather than the impoverishment of the maternal sphere.

Plotting Coincidence

Barely developed in *Blithedale*, this alternative rendering of the maternal as (performative) subjectivity rather than (originary) space centrally informs *The Lamplighter*. In Maria Susanna Cummins's novel, the mother's constitution as origin is identified as a *consequence* of the paternal interdiction of her body, which effects her *displacement* from historical time. In the mode of the feminist fetishist, the novel's orphaned heroine disavows the loss, not of a pre-historical maternal plenitude—on the contrary, the mother's fluidity, her diffusive presence, is figured in the novel as the result of her body's *mutilation*—but of maternal authority, and the intersubjective relations it structures. What Gertrude refuses to renounce is an extra-patriarchal sociality, a mode of "familiar intercourse," external to the logic of pre-oedipal complementarity and oedipal subjectivity alike. Where "familiar intercourse" obtains, historically contingent affinities (or sympathies) determine the configurations of the familial, rather than the reverse, than the regulation of affinities in and by a naturalized familial economy.

A series of "strange coincidence[s]" and repetitions functions to reinstate this alternative intersubjective mode, to restore to each other the characters separated by the inauguration of the paternal prohibition. The linchpin of this iterative plot is Gertrude, whom we first encounter in an abandoned state, hungry, ragged and cold; in the formulation of her uncharitable caretaker, who has just turned the child out of doors, Gertrude is "the city's property," one of "[t]hem children that come into the world nobody knows how" and "don't get out of it in a hurry."[18] *The Lamplighter* thus tracks Gertrude, not in the fashion of the standard female *bildungsroman,* from the scene of her origins to her acquisition of normative femininity (as is true, for instance, of Ellen Montgomery in Susan Warner's *The Wide, Wide World*), but rather from *object status* to gendered subjectivity, or more precisely, from a non-originary social non-existence (as "the city's property") to a hybrid position, as both True Woman *and* the keeper of the "phallic" mother's censored sociality. Driven out into the winter street, Gertrude finds shelter with the aptly named Trueman Flint, an old lamplighter she was accustomed to trail on his nightly rounds. More to the point, Trueman Flint is an exemplary reader (or auditor) of the sentimental text, who as often as he hears Gertrude tell her tale of grief, can "never [hear it] *without crying*" (*L* 33), and so adopts the child he is so ill-equipped to raise to Womanhood, less by reason of his gender than of his social class. Sensitive to his own deficiencies, Trueman Flint enlists the aid of Emily Graham, a wealthy "blind girl," who assumes the expense of Gertrude's care and, more significantly, assumes in Gertrude's life the place of the missing (good, middle-class, Christian) mother.

That this "girl" so readily supplies the missing maternal affect results at least as much from her blindness, as this condition is represented in the narrative, as from her abundance of Christian sentiment or her as yet concealed relation to Gertrude's father, Phillip, which comes to light only at the novel's end. Emily's blindness effects a de-formation, or dissolution, of her corporeal and subjective boundaries and thereby locates her beyond (or prior to) the visual dialectic of intersubjectivity. Unable to return the gaze, to see the other seeing her, Emily becomes the locus of her interlocutor's self-completion. Thus Gertrude positively delights, at least initially, in her discovery of Emily's blindness, which, from

Gertrude's point of view, only perfects Emily's capacity for sentimental communion.

> "Not see!" said Gerty; "can't you see anything? Can't you see me now?"
> "No," said Miss Graham.
> "O!" exclaimed Gerty, drawing a long breath, "*I'm so glad.*"
> "Glad!" said Miss Graham, in the saddest voice that ever was heard.
> "O, yes!" said Gerty, "so glad you can't see me!—because now, per-
> haps, you'll love me." (*L* 54)

If on one level Emily's blindness permits her to supply the place
of the missing mother in Gertrude's life, on another level Gertrude
is quick to interrogate the mother's liminal position in the dominant cultural narrative of subject formation. When she considers
from Emily's vantage the mother's debarrment from this privileged
dimension of symbolic exchange (*the* dimension, in Lacan's account, of the recognition of desire), Gertrude promptly disclaims
the pleasures of a filial coherence predicated on the mother's rup-
tural relation to knowledge and authority, on her confinement to
what Michel Chion has termed the darkness of the "uterine
night."[19]

> "But just think, Gerty," said Emily, in the same sad voice, "how you
> would feel if you could not see the light, could not see anything in the
> world?"
> "Can't you see the sun, and the stars, and the sky, and the church
> we're in? Are you in the dark?"
> "In the dark, all the time, day and night in the dark."
> Gerty burst into a paroxysm of tears. "O!" exclaimed she, as soon as
> she could find voice amid the sobs, "it's too bad! it's too bad!"
> The child's grief was contagious; and, for the first time for years, Emily
> wept bitterly for her blindness. . . .
> "I shouldn't be happy in the dark; I should hate to be!" said Gerty. "I
> an't glad you're blind; I'm real sorry. I wish you could see me and every-
> thing." (*L* 54–55)

The circumstances of Emily's blinding further specify the relation
between blindness and motherhood that transforms Gertrude's

grief at Emily's consignment to the dark into a tacit critique of the mother's placement in/as the pre-history of the subject. As the plot unfolds, we learn that Emily is blinded when "a powerful acid" leaves its imprint on her flesh, in a scenario that plainly casts her as the object of an oedipal contest (L 320). The unwitting perpetrator proves to be none other than Gertrude's father and Emily's adoptive brother, Phillip, who, having been raised together with Emily and enjoyed with her a "constant freedom and familiarity of inter- course," aspires at last to take her as his wife (L 372). Always averse to his stepson, and doubly so since the death of Phillip's mother (Mr. Graham's second wife), Emily's father thwarts the match, claiming that Phillip has committed forgery—has forged the pater- nal name in order to defraud Mr. Graham of his wealth. Witness to this conflict between (step)father and (step)son, Emily moves to intercede, but faints in distress before she is able to speak. Think- ing to revive her, Phillip reaches for a bottle of cologne, but in his outrage at Mr. Graham's unjustified accusation, seizes the wrong vial and spills its corrosive contents, putting out Emily's eyes. At stake in this dislocated, or defamiliarized, oedipal conflict—which nevertheless reads as straightforwardly oedipal the moment we place Emily into the position of Phillip's *mother*—is a rescripting of the pre-oedipal and of the mother's relation to history and (inter)subjectivity. By substituting a stepsister for the mother, and a stepbrother for the son, Cummins produces a version of oedipal strife that implicitly contests the father's rights of possession over the mother's body (contests the mother's castration, or symbolic dispossession) and its corollary, the mother's ejection from history as an originary body. More specifically, by refiguring the mother- son relation as a relation between adoptive siblings, Cummins le- gitimates the "son's" desire to retain a relation to the "mother" unmediated by paternal authority; Mr. Graham is seen to exert arbitrary control over an affinity that is neither founded on, nor vio- lates, "nature." Furthermore, Cummins suggests that the "mother's" status as the site of an (originary) complementarity (in this context, her blindness) follows, not from nature, but from the paternal pro-

hibition on her body; it is Phillip, acting under the weight of paternal law, who strips the mother of the "phallus," throws her off the
axis of the (recognition of) desire, relegates her to the phantasmatic.
If for Ruth Mack Brunswick phallic motherhood is projected back
onto the mother-in-the-dyad, here originary motherhood is
retroactively imposed on the body of the "phallic" mother (the
mother in/of "familiar intercourse").

As a result of her blinding, of her transformation from a subject
into a(n archaic or anterior) space, "familiar intercourse" with
Emily is in turn reconceived as a modality of *pre-symbolic* communion. Before her blinding sets "a fatal seal . . . to all [her] earthly
hopes" (*L* 321), Emily's "free and familiar intercourse" with Phillip
turns on their "mutual dependence" (*L* 314), marked by a kind of
code-switching, a crossing of gendered behaviors. Thus Phillip's is
"the leading spirit, the strong and determined will" (*L* 314), but his
"manly voice" articulates a "woman's depth of feeling, warmth of
heart, and sympathizing sweetness of manner" (*L* 318). Conversely, Emily submits to her "bold young protector and ruler," but
Phillip's rule proves absolutely contingent on Emily's successful ne-
gotiation of phallic authority, on her capacity to deflect from
Phillip Mr. Graham's gaze of "suspicion and dislike" (*L* 315). With
Phillip's accession to paternal law, Emily reduces to an embodiment of the Father's message:

> None could live in familiar intercourse with Emily, listen to her words,
> observe the radiance of her heavenly smile, and breathe in the pure at-
> mosphere that environed her very being, and not carry away with them
> the love of virtue and holiness, if not something of their essence. (*L* 240)

In this version of "familiar intercourse," the division in and of the
speaking subject dissolves, so that Emily's interlocutors inhabit the
place of the m/other. Conceived as an "environ[ment]," rather than
a speaking subject, "Emily" remains at once prior to the production of meaning ("her" meaning is not articulated, but inhaled)
and essentially subordinate to the Father's law (to the precepts of

patriarchal religion). This (re)constitution of the "mother" as pre-
historical body sends Phillip to sea, to wander the globe in the
posture of a "grieved and tired child" (L 275). His affecting
"melancholy" elicits the love of the ship captain's frail daughter,
who bears Phillip's daughter and promptly succumbs to cholera;
and it eventually moves Gertrude herself to tears, even before the
identity of this returning traveler is known to her.

Against this scenario, Gertrude practices a kind of feminist
fetishism, refusing to acknowledge the loss of the mother as the
subject of an extra- or (more precisely) counter-patriarchal "familiar intercourse." In this frame, what Gertrude disavows is less
the mother's inscription as lack, than her inscription as plenitude—
her blindness.

> [Gertrude's] large eyes were fixed upon Emily's face, which always
> seemed, in some unaccountable way, to fascinate the little girl; so at-
> tentively did she watch the play of the features in a countenance the
> charm of which many an older person than Gerty had felt, but tried in
> vain to describe. It was not beauty,—at least not brilliant beauty,—for
> that Emily had not possessed. . . . It was not compassion for her blind-
> ness, though so great a misfortune might well, and always did, excite the
> warmest sympathy. But it was hard to realize that Emily *was* blind. (L 64)

While Cummins goes on to attribute the difficulty of recognizing
Emily's condition to her peaceful resignation, her modest refusal
to call attention to her plight, this passage begins, at any rate, as a
kind of meditation on Gertrude's "fascinat[ion]" with Emily. Working backward, then, through the turns in the narration, which di-
verted us from the initial focus on *Gertrude's* fixation, to the
consideration of *other people's* perceptions of Emily and finally to
a lengthy celebration of *Emily's* selflessness, we see that the disinclination to acknowledge Emily's blindness logically belongs to
Gertrude—as the cause of her fascinated gaze. By disavowing
Emily's blindness, Gertrude reconnects her to the "world," (re)in-
serts her in historical time.

> . . . Miss Graham found that in Gertrude's observing eyes, and her feel-
> ing and glowing descriptions of everything that came within their gaze,
> she was herself renewing acquaintance with the outside world. (L 108)
> [By] earnest and unsparing efforts to bring her much-loved friend into
> communion with everything she herself enjoyed, [Gertrude] had called
> into play faculties which blindness had rendered almost dormant, and
> become what Uncle True bade her, eyes to her benefactor. (L 128)

More particularly, Gertrude restores Emily as the subject of her censored "intercourse" with Phillip, by mediating Phillip's return. In a wildly improbable sequence of events, whose implausibility Cummins is only too glad to concede, Phillip comes home to his native New England to search out his daughter, only to find her in "familiar intercourse" with none other than his long-lost "sister." "O, strange coincidence! O, righteous retribution!" Phillip avers, imagining himself now prohibited from daughter and "sister" alike, "which at the very moment when I was picturing to myself the consummation of my cherished hopes, crushed me once more beneath the iron hand of a destiny that would not be cheated of its victim" (L 389). Under Gertrude's careful instruction, however, Phillip learns to disavow his destiny, to disbelieve in the "iron hand" of paternal law, and thus finds himself reunited with Emily at the novel's close, while a defeated Mr. Graham takes up his cry: "Singular coincidence! Very singular! Very!" (L 400).

In their fetishizing of Emily, Gertrude and Phillip invest her with symbolic authority and historical specificity in the face of a symbolic that relegates her to nature, as the originary ground of the bourgeois social subject. At the same time, *The Lamplighter*'s conclusion registers the fundamental duplicity of the fetishist's disavowal, which *refuses*, without necessarily *displacing*, the existing relations of power. Thus, while Phillip persuades Emily to wed, and thereby extracts her at last from her father's house, Emily agrees only reluctantly, out of deference to Phillip's desire. Perceiving that she is soon to depart this world for her "Father's home," the blind girl's "last, best work" is to "cast a ray from her

blessed spirit into [Phillip's] darkened soul," mediating this time
not Phillip's resistance, but his subjection to paternal law (L 421).
If Gertrude and Phillip escape the social opprobrium that Grosz's
lesbian fetishist incurs, their recoding of the domestic as the site
of denaturalized "fraternal" relations remains partial, provisional.
As though in retreat from the obliquely incestuous arrangement
with which the requirement to end in marriage has left her, Cummins asserts Emily's paternal orientation against the force of filial
desire.

But the status of the mother at the novel's close does not hinge
entirely on Emily's destiny, inasmuch as Gertrude is herself a participant in an ambiguously fraternal relation. Raised together with
the son of Trueman Flint's widowed neighbor, Gertrude enters into
her equivalent of "free and familiar intercourse" with Willie, in a
relation uncomplicated this time by the censoring presence of a
father, though interrupted by the requirement that Willie function
as a man, seeking his fortunes in the sphere of international com-
merce. It is Gertrude's fear, confided to Emily, that Willie, departed
for employment abroad, is forever lost to her, which leads Emily
to remark on the other improbability that structures the novel's
discourse:

> . . . Emily wept as she listened, and when Gertrude had finished she
> pressed her again and again to her heart, exclaiming, as she did so, with
> an excitement of tone and manner which Gertrude had never before wit-
> nessed in the usually calm and placid blind girl, "Strange, strange, that
> you, too, should thus be doomed!" (L 313)

Unaware at this point that Phillip has returned, believing him
in fact to be dead, Emily reads in their shared grief for a lost
"brother" their common "doom." However, Willie returns to wed
Gertrude, just as Phillip reappears to implore Emily's hand, so
that, Mr. Graham's muttered cry notwithstanding, the novel frames
in and as a repetition the "singular" event on which it hinges.
Gertrude not only restores Phillip to Emily, but also sees her own

displaced "brother" reinstated in a relation of "familiar inter-course," which by virtue of its resemblance to Emily's and Phillip's "free" relation would tend to attribute Emily's (maternal) subjec-tivity to Gertrude. Rather than a non-iterable improbability, "coin-cidence" names the temporality of a feminist fetishism, of the desire for a phallically invested female subject, which pits itself against the likely and the known, in plain defiance of the odds.

5 "Your Mother Is Here"

Harriet Jacobs and the Decommodification of Motherhood

> The structure of unreality that the black woman
> must confront originates in the historical moment
> when language ceases to speak, the historical
> moment at which hierarchies of power (even the
> ones to which some women belong) simply run out
> of terms because the empowered meets in the black
> female the veritable nemesis of degree and difference.
> —Hortense Spillers

> As one goes down the grotesquely mistranscribed
> names of these women, the sacrificed widows, in
> the police reports included in the records of the East
> India Company, one cannot put together a "voice. . .".
> Faced with the dialectically interlocking sentences
> that are constructible as "White men are saving brown
> women from brown men" and "The women wanted to
> die," the postcolonial woman intellectual asks the
> question of simple semiosis—What does this mean?
> —and begins to plot a history.
> —Gayatri Chakravorty Spivak

Harriet Jacobs's importation into *Incidents in the Life of a Slave Girl* of the sentimental novel's conventions functions for several critics of the text as the mark both of her confinement in a dominant cultural discourse of feminine gender *and* of her (sub)textual resistance to it, a resistance that operates between the lines, making audible what Hortense Spillers calls the "interstice," the missing or unspoken word that is the black woman in, and in the wake of, her captivity.[1] Eliding the complex metaphorics of Spillers's term, however, readers of Jacobs's text typically locate the black female subject in the register of experience. As Hazel Carby puts it, "the narrative of Linda Brent's life stands as an exposition of her womanhood and motherhood contradicting and transforming an ideology that could not take account of her experience."[2] Valerie Smith echoes Carby on this point, suggesting that Jacobs "seized authority over her literary restraints in much the same way that she seized power in life. From within her ellipses and ironies—linguistic narrow spaces—she expresses the complexity of her experience as a black woman."[3] Smith finally emphasizes the "limitations" of "this tactic," claiming that Jacobs's recourse to the sentimental "trivializes the complexity of her situation,"[4] while Carby credits as more fully transformative the effects of Jacobs's discursive appropriation. But the point is that for both critics, Jacobs (re)figures feminine gender as a racialized sign system by her invocation of sentimental discourse as what *fails* to accommodate the *"experience"* of black women. Focusing for the moment on Carby's and Smith's rhetorical tactics, I remark that "experience" ambiguously designates both a *limit* (where a dominant gender discourse breaks off its accounting) and a *location* (the ground of the black female subject). As a result, this reading of Jacobs cuts two ways. In one sense, Carby and Smith may be seen to define the black woman's "experience" as something itself structured by the order of signifiers (in other words, they may be seen to assume, with Gayatri Spivak, that "sign-structure[s] operate experience"),[5] so that the black woman's experience would refer to her confrontation with a "structure of unreality" that leaves her unspoken, with the history of her inscription as "the principal point of passage between the human and the non-human world."[6] From this vantage, the black woman would appear as the subject of her historically determined difference, whom we confront in her deviation from the discourses of feminine gender and race that reduce her to silence and non-being. At the same time, Carby's and Smith's formulations lend themselves to the quite different proposition that "experience" is prior to the discourses that fail in their accounting of it, and as such would designate the outside of a sign-structure, where we recuperate the black female subject in her full "complexity." On this assumption, the critic peels away the dominant discourses of gender and race, and listens for the black woman to tell it like it is.

While neither Carby's nor Smith's reading of Jacobs is given over to such a positivist construction of black women's identity, I point to this fault-line in their formulations, to their flirtation with the more essentialist resonances of "experience" in both its Marxist and feminist critical contexts, as an index to the difficulty of what both Spillers and Spivak propose: an articulation of the missing word, and/as the cerning of a lexical absence that neither veils a prediscursive presence, nor liquidates its referent (as though, lacking a name, the black woman would simply cease to exist), but rather marks with a silence the historical site of a violent erasure. Thus to articulate the missing term is neither to restore the lost object, to summon her forward into discourse, nor is it to concede the historically determined limits of discourse as the limit of cultural intelligibility. Rather, to articulate the missing term is to interrogate the modes of the symbolic and political production of the unspeakable, to take as one's object the practices of boundary-making.

More particularly, I suggest that "experience" signifies in Spillers's text not a space, or set of phenomena that we might *map,* but a *condition*; "experience" refers us precisely to the phantasmatic nature of social-symbolic topographies. In this view, "experience" is neither "outside" discourse (as prediscursive ground), nor "inside" it (as an effect of discourse, subordinate to the power of the namer), since it is what interrupts or defers the trajectory of the spatial metaphor, what intervenes to prevent the understanding of discourse as continuous real space. "Experience" thus makes any particular discursive reality legible in its incompletion, as a "structure of unreality." Spillers invokes "experience" this way:

... the first order of symbolic business within a community is the articulation of what we would call a first-order naming, words that express the experience of the community in diachronic time, in daily social relationships, in economic well-being, in the identity of a self. A second order of naming, or words about the first order, would articulate another level of symbolic responses. . . . The literature of African-Americans . . . constitute[s] a second . . . order of naming with the potential power to become a first order, to the degree that the community and the writer sustain a mutual engagement that leads to seeing anew in both. Since the content concerning the actual life experiences of black women is barely articulated, to say nothing of exhausted, we are in the incredible position of having either to create a first-order discourse on black women's community, and/or speak immediately into the void left by its absence. . . .[7]

To the extent that it escapes articulation in a a first-order discourse, black women's experience registers itself at the level of second-order discourse (of "words about the first order") as "the void," as a gap in the discourses of gender and race that betrays their partiality, their structural disarticulations. At the level of first-order discourse, black women's "experience" is a *product* of its under-articulation, in the sense that to create a first-order discourse on black women's community would not be simply to record what *is*, but to alter the "experience" of "daily social relationships." Spillers's insistence that the writer alone cannot produce first-order discourse, in the absence of a "mutual engagement" with the community that would result in a collective new perception of "experience," suggests that "experience" can only be thought in relation to the recognized possibilities and limitations of symbolizing it. From this perspective, the "experience" of the community debarred from the symbolic is the "experience" of that debarment; the experience of "daily social relationships" for which the legitimized cultural discourses supply no name, so that in order to signify these relationships the participants must strategize and improvise (and, in so doing, must risk alerting the empowered, who will often rename and pathologize what such symbolization makes visible); the "experience" of an economic well-being necessarily di-

minished to the extent that the community's economic interests go
un- or misnamed in the capitalist marketplace.[8] If black women's
"experience" is a product of its under-articulation, however, at the
level of second-order discourse, the unspoken of the community's
"experience" reappears as a *remainder,* or excess, as a silence that
underwrites but also interrupts the dominant discourses of social
and political legitimation. The un- or under-articulated "life experiences of black women" announce the failure in and of the
discourses of race and gender to coincide with, or "fully" account
for, the (un)realities they generate.

If we read Jacobs's unaccounted or unarticulated experience in
this light, as signifying the particular, historical, non-innocent
relation of a radically dehumanized subject to discourse and
empowerment, the "Subaltern Studies" model Spivak engages
becomes useful for considering the question of Jacobs's "tactics"
and their efficacy. This is not to overlook the specificity of the postcolonial context to which this model speaks and which Spivak, at
any rate, quite forcefully distinguishes from a "first-world context,"
and the conditions of the production of a "poor, black and female"
subject in the U.S. For Spivak this difference hinges on "the
necessary stratification of colonial subject constitution," which
"makes 'color' useless as an emancipatory signifier."[9] Thus, Spivak
suggests, the radical class differences among indigenous women on
the Indian subcontinent would render the term "women of color"
a meaningless political rallying point. While I would argue that the
distinction between first world and postcolonial contexts cannot
be reduced to the presence or absence of stratification, or, in other
words, that issues of class stratification are by no means irrelevant
to the category "women of color" in the U.S. today (even if the
class lines are differently configured in this first-world context),
Spivak's caution about the kind of transposition of models I am
making here turns out to be quite appropriate with respect to the
social and political economies of slavery, where it makes no sense
to speak of class stratification among a captive black population.
If, as Spillers argues, there can be no gender in the absence of

subjectivity, so that the radically commodified black body is effectively ungendered, then it seems clear as well that there are no distinctions of social class within a class of people juridically constituted as property.[10] But inasmuch as the point of the Subaltern Studies model is to enable us to think a particular kind of exclusion from the symbolic, I will argue that the model is nevertheless pertinent to the conditions of the African-American in, and in the aftermath, of her 250-year captivity. The model is also pertinent to a consideration of my own position as a member of a predominantly white intellectual first-world elite. Because it marks (makes visible) the position of the (elite) critic as well as of the (subaltern) text, this model requires me to engage the proposition that the "Other as subject is inaccessible" to me.[11]

Central to the intellectual's plotting of a subaltern "history," in Spivak's analysis, is a construction of the subaltern as a differential subject. Subaltern Studies defines the "subaltern classes" or "people" as "the demographic difference between the total Indian population and all those whom we have described as the 'elite.'" Thus the "subaltern classes" represent an "ideal category," comprised in the abstract of all those who do *not* belong to "dominant foreign groups" or "dominant indigenous groups," at either the "all-India" or "regional and local" levels.[12] Furthermore, the category of "the regional elite-subaltern," which constitutes a kind of "floating buffer zone" between those elite groups empowered at the national level and the non-elite, are themselves differentially defined in their "deviation" from the latter, "ideal" category.[13] That is, the "subaltern classes" are defined as the non-elite, while the "regional elite-subaltern" are defined in their *difference* from this *differential* ideal, as the not non-elite. What interests me here, as particularly relevant to Jacobs's narrative, is this constitution of the elite-subaltern subject in and as a double negation that does not reduce to an affirmation. Locating Jacobs in this intermediate zone, I want to consider that she speaks to the white "women of the North,"[14] her designated readers, not as the subject in and of a dominant discourse, but rather as a not-commodity; more particularly, as a not non-woman who does not, however, resolve into elite womanhood.[15]

In order to unpack this claim, I will rewrite the hierarchy of elite, elite-subaltern, and subaltern non-elite that informs the work of Subaltern Studies as follows:

    1. White men |— elite
    2. White women |
    3. Literate, emancipated (or fugitive) black men and women.
    4. Black people in captivity.

Here the categories or positions in this social hierarchy are generated, not by the interplay of race and class, but by that of race and gender. I shift the emphasis *away* from class because in a slave economy, and for the purposes of such broad schematizations, race implies class in precisely the ways that, as Spivak emphasizes, it does not in the colonial and postcolonial frames. Blackness means subaltern status. Conversely, whiteness means at a minimum locally empowered, or elite-subaltern status. (As chapter XII of Jacobs's narrative, "Fear of Insurrection," reminds us, the most underprivileged Southern whites constitute a regional elite-subaltern class, with power of domination over the captive black, and existing in a highly charged and unstable relation to the regional elite-subaltern/emancipated black, as exemplified in the text by Linda Brent's grandmother.) I shift the emphasis *toward* gender in order to graft the implications of Spillers's claim onto the Subaltern Studies model: to signify that gender does not function comparably at every level of this hierarchy. For Spillers, the radical commodification of the black body in slavery subtracts it from the logic of gendered identity by unmaking "the body" as such. The captive black body is systematically stripped of social determination to expose something "vestibular" to culture, to "the body," what Spillers calls "the flesh." Under these circumstances, gender is reduced to its Euro-American articulation and the subaltern woman finds herself not (as in Spivak's example) in the in-between of a dominant foreign and an indigenous local construction of feminine gender, but in the in-between of a dominant gender construction and an objectification so radical it ungenders. Thus the literate, emancipated African-American elite-subaltern stands not only in a vexed relation to the symbolic, as a not unspoken subject, but in a vexed relation to gender, as a not ungendered object. And while in the scenario Spivak outlines in the epigraph, a foreign elite and an indigenous regional elite dispute the legitimacy of subaltern gender constructions, in Jacobs's text it is *elite,* Euro-American gender construction that will offer a site, or focus, for a *subaltern* revision of existing power relations.

Simultaneously inscribing herself in the sentimental discourse of feminine gender, and marking it as the site of her underarticulation, Jacobs performs a double action. I will argue that she rewrites her status as commodity through accession to white feminine gender, and rewrites feminine gender from the vantage of the not-commodity—of a decommodified female subject. The idea of "decommodification" usefully locates this subject in the movement from commodity to subject status, a movement, moreover, in which both positions, that of the commodity and of the subject, become legible as "structures of unreality."[16] The decommodified subject thus brings her unspoken difference to bear on the elite identities she assumes (of woman; of author) by signifying their partiality, their status as intelligible only within a specific and historically contingent structure of empowerment. More particularly, I want to consider how the decommodified black mother disarticulates essentialized white motherhood, and the sentimental discourse of maternal love. *Incidents* offers a subaltern rewriting of the "dialectically interlocking sentences" which I construct as follows: "Motherhood is a natural function, prior to language, history and identity" and "The black female's reproduction increases the white man's property." Jacobs at once legitimates her claim to her children in the discourse of natural maternal affinity *and* denaturalizes elite motherhood, which emerges in her text as a culturally specific, performative and contested identity.

Where does Jacobs's subaltern writing position me, a middle-class white feminist, whose larger cultural and historical preroga-

tive it has been to fill in my black "sisters"' silences; an academic
trained in the Euro-American production of knowledges, in ways
that remain inevitably determining of how I ask Spivak's "question
of simple semiosis"? In Spivak's formulation, the elite reader of the
subaltern text needs first to acknowledge and refuse the twin possibilities of "listen[ing] to" or "speak[ing] for" the muted subject, of
(re)constructing her voice out of her silences. Instead, Spivak
elaborates an alternative critical practice, which she distinguishes
as "speaking to" the subaltern subject. In distinction to "speaking
for," "speaking to" does not reduce to a gesture of retrieval or re-
covery, since what is spoken to are structures of domination as they
function to produce subaltern status. Thus to "speak to" the historically muted subject is to take seriously the proposition that the
subaltern subject has been muted, and for that reason and to that
degree remains inaccessible as subject to the readers of her text.
The project is to consider how specific discourses generate the conditions of the subaltern subject's existence and "not simply [to]
substitut[e] the lost figure of the colonized."[17] When I "speak to"
the subaltern subject, I critique the relations of power that engender her, so that the "object" of my interrogation becomes my
own privilege, and the construction of alterity on which that privilege is founded.

> When we come to the concomitant question of the consciousness of
> the subaltern, the notion of what the work *cannot* say becomes impor-
> tant. . . . "The subject" implied by the texts of insurgency can only
> serve as a counterpossibility for the narrative sanctions granted to the
> colonial subject in the dominant groups. The postcolonial intellectuals
> learn that their privilege is their loss.[18]

My project here is to speak to the emergence in Jacobs's text of
such a "counterpossibility" for the "narrative sanctions granted"
the mid-nineteenth-century white female author (of sentimental
fiction) and the late-twentieth-century white feminist theorist (of
the affective maternal body). This "counterpossibility" is *not* ren-

dered in the form of an elaborated oppositional discourse, of which Harriet Jacobs would be the identifiable subject. Rather, the "counterpossibility" is the product of Jacobs's silences as they intervene in the dominant social, juridical, and political discourses of race and gender, in such a way as to render unintelligible any foundationalist claim to the *a priori* status of the reproductive female body.

The "Tangled Skeins" of Genealogy: The Children, the Doctor, His Slave, and Her Lover

Narrating the event of her daughter's baptism, Jacobs articulates the impossibility of naming the infant, in the absence of the legitimated kinship relations that would confer social identity.

> When my baby was about to be christened, the former mistress of my father stepped up to me, and proposed to give it her Christian name. To this I added the surname of my father, who had himself no legal right to it; for my grandfather on the paternal side was a white gentleman. What tangled skeins are the genealogies of slavery! I loved my father; but it mortified me to be obliged to bestow his name on my children. (*I* 78)

While the final sentence of this passage might be read, out of context, as the painful admission of the (generic) unwed mother, with only her maiden name to confer on her progeny, what is at issue here, of course, is not Linda Brent's failure to circulate as an object of exchange within a patriarchal economy of marriage, but rather the absolute degree of her appropriation by the subject of patriarchal power.[19] In context, the shame of conferring her own father's name hinges at least as much on the fact that it is not *his* (legal) name, as that it should, properly speaking, no longer be *hers*. Her father can no more identify her, than she her child, as the intervention in the naming process of his "former mistress" serves implicitly to underscore. Yet Jacobs's insistence here on a multigenerational interpretive frame serves more subtly to figure the baptism, not only as a vexed occasion for the naming of property, but more particularly for the naming of property that at least partially negates its owner's entitlement. Under other circumstances, her children might, like Brent's father, have assumed the name of their white progenitor, which although not their "own," would certainly have been no less so than the illegally assumed surname of an unknown great-grandfather; in fact, the father of Brent's children has explicitly authorized her to bestow his name. But inasmuch as she foils her master's sexual advances—contests his unconditional title to her body—by taking *another* white man as her lover, Brent "dare[s] not while my master lived" confer the name of the master's white rival on the children who (by virtue of their mother's condition) nonetheless remain her master's alienable possession. The tangled genealogy that transforms naming into an improvisational act is further complicated here by the commodity's resistance. If, as a result, her children are not the mark of her objectification, but rather, as she styles them, a negation of the slave's social death, a "link to life," they are a link that remains, as such, unrepresentable/under-represented.

The contradictions and (un)realities that structure the act of naming her children structure as well the representation of her relation to them. Motherhood is neither simply the inscription of her captive "condition" on her children (in which case their names are of no importance), nor simply the inscription of her shamed femininity (in which case her children are unambiguously bastards, whose names are better left unspoken). Rather, Linda Brent's motherhood constitutes an act of subaltern insurgency, the product of her refusal to submit to coerced sexual relations with her master. It is Brent's "identity" as a mother that governs what I have proposed to call a narrative of decommodification, both in the sense that the birth of her children inaugurates the drive for their emancipation and her own, and because the contradictions of elite-subaltern status (of existence as a not non-elite) become legible specifically with reference to the discursive constructions of motherhood. How does the narrative engender a motherhood that reduces neither to a natural function, nor to the reproduction of property—or in other words, how does it engender a motherhood that inhabits neither the symbolic economy of gender in pre-abolition America, nor that of race? I want first to consider the "tactics" Jacobs employs to mark the sentimental discourse of motherhood as inadequate. Given its understanding of motherhood as an essentially socializing/moral influence, sentimentalism can only indict the fallen woman for a breach of social good form that marks her as unnatural.

Within the terms of sentimental discourse, then, the conditions of Brent's motherhood would delegitimate her status as a mother; only the hyperbolic display of naturalized maternal qualities, humility, sacrifice, and constant devotion to her children, might earn her remittance of this sin. However, in the chapter entitled, sentimentally, "The Confession," Brent's daughter Ellen counters the logic of this essentialized motherhood, refusing to figure her connection to her mother as natural (original; ineffable), prior to knowledge and identity, and equally refusing to construct as unnatural (monstrous; unspeakable) her mother's illicit sexual past. Significantly, it is by prohibiting her mother's confession, by imposing silence, that she contends for the meaning of what therefore remains unspoken.

> I recounted my early sufferings in slavery, and told her how nearly they had crushed me. I began to tell her how they had driven me into a great sin, when she clasped me in her arms and exclaimed, "O, don't mother! Please don't tell me anymore."
>
> I said, "But, my child, I want you to know about your father."
>
> "I know all about it mother," she replied; "I am nothing to my father, and he is nothing to me. All my love is for you. . . . He never spoke to me as he did to his little Fanny. I knew all the time he was my father, for Fanny's nurse told me so; but she said I must never tell any body, and I never did. I used to wish he would take me in his arms, as he did Fanny. . . . I thought if he was my own father, he ought to love me. I was a little girl then, and didn't know any better. But now I never think any thing about my father. All my love is for you." She hugged me closer as she

spoke, and I thanked God that the knowledge I had so much dreaded to
impart had not diminished the affection of my child. I had not the
slightest idea that she knew that portion of my history. . . . But I loved
the dear girl better for the delicacy she had manifested towards her
unfortunate mother. (*I* 188-89)

Pronounced in the exclamatory style of sentimental melodrama,
Ellen's injunction against telling glosses silence as a mark of feminine discretion or "delicacy," a reading her mother makes explicit
in the final line of this passage. The framing of this aborted con-
fessional moment, then, (if not its actual content) conforms to a
sentimental paradigm, in which Ellen "delicately" spares her
mother the abasement of articulating a shameful sexual past. By
sparing her mother the ordeal of confession, the illegitimate
daughter might legitimate her mother as a woman for whom confession would be an ordeal—legitimate her on the ground that she
deems her own history unspeakable. However, when Ellen proceeds to assure her mother that she is already in possession of the
knowledge her mother would disclose, the circumstances Ellen rehearses are not exactly the thing which feminine "delicacy" would
enjoin us to veil. What stands in as the cause of a necessary silence
in Ellen's account is no longer an illicit sexual connection that
cannot with propriety be repeated, but an experience of non-being
that can signify its enormity only in the failures of discourse to
account for it.[20] "I am nothing to my father," she asserts of her
relation to her mother's lover (who has at this point in the narrative purchased the children, to become master as well as father),
or in other words, to him she is only a thing, not a daughter (like
Fanny), or a woman. "[A]nd," she continues, effectively rewriting
her object status, "he is nothing to me." Her father is not anything
a father is said to be, and in a stunning gesture that passes as a
simple flair for rhetorical symmetry, the *slave* expels the *master*
from the domain of signifiable subject positions: he is only a thing
to me. Ellen's acknowledgment of her unspeakable origins thus
shifts the "site" of the unspoken: rather than invoke her mother's

sexual history, Ellen invokes their shared history of being nothing/a thing, and of constituting oneself in a refusal of object status that is not, however, an accession to discursive subjectivity.

Asserting that her father is nothing to her, Ellen defines herself in a negation of her social non-being, as a not non-woman. In this frame, she gives herself over to her mother—"All my love is for you"—not on the basis of a natural affinity that precedes the contingency, or conditionality, of historical relationships, but with reference to a common experience of social relations of power. Thus she constructs her kinship to her mother as something that postdates her inscription in the symbolic—depends on her "know[ing] . . . better." By marking her kinship to her mother with an injunction to silence, articulated in the very sentimental idiom that fails her, Ellen locates the mother-daughter bond in a shared, subaltern relation to this dominant gender discourse.

The scene of Brent's averted "confession" is thus inhabited by an under-articulated counternarrative of motherhood, structured in, and in resistance to, the very fact of the black mother's conditionality. As such, Ellen's relation to her mother stands in contrast to Brent's own, which precedes and cannot accommodate the daughter's knowledge.

> I was born a slave; but I never knew it till six years of happy childhood had passed away. . . . [My parents] lived together in a comfortable home; and though we were all slaves, I was so fondly shielded that I never dreamed I was a piece of merchandise, trusted to them for safe keeping, and liable to be demanded of them at any moment. . . When I was six years old my mother died; and then, for the first time, I learned, by the talk around me, that I was a slave. (*I* 5-6)

In her representation of this relation, Jacobs again resists any simple reduction of the captive mother to her "condition," to the radical loss of identity she confers on her offspring; Linda Brent here assumes the non-identity of the slave only with her mother's loss. But this inversion of terms, that transforms the captive mother from the origin (or cause) of the slave's loss of identity, into that which is lost at the origin—from the moment of the inception of the slave's self-consciousness—precisely reproduces the dehistoricizing logic of sentimental discourse. Here motherhood occupies an imaginary zone, anterior to the infant's recognition of power relations; by extension, the child's inscription in the symbolic is marked by the mother's death.

Being There

In the frame of both scenarios, of Linda Brent's unconditional relation to her mother and her historically conditioned relation to her daughter, I read, as a subaltern intervention in the discourse of naturalized motherhood, Jacobs's representation of her seven-year confinement in the crawl space above her grandmother's storeroom. If, in the representation of Brent's relation to her daughter, Jacobs insists on the specificity of the commodity's experience as it counters the discourse of naturalized motherhood, conversely, in the representation of Brent's crippling confinement, she engages the discourse of naturalized motherhood to underwrite the decommodification of the captive maternal body. At the risk of an over-schematization, I suggest that in "The Confession" Jacobs activates the second proposition, "motherhood is the reproduction of property," in order to rewrite the first, "motherhood is a natural function"; while in "The Loophole of Retreat," she activates the first in order to rewrite the second. "The Loophole" represents an insurgent elaboration of a possibility glimpsed but not developed in Jacobs's construction of Brent's relation to her mother: the subaltern revision of the imaginary zone of bourgeois motherhood.

Because she finds herself increasingly without alternatives in the face of her master's continued sexual coercions, and can discern no actual possibility of flight, Brent resolves to *stage* her escape to the north. Suspecting that her owner, Dr. Flint, only retains possession of the children in order to blackmail her, she gambles that by her disappearance she will dupe him into selling the children to their father. Brent strategically "retreats," first, briefly, into the attic of a sympathizing white woman, and then into the suffocating space above her grandmother's shed. Houston Baker has aptly characterized this "retreat" as an "interiorization and enclosure equivalent to burial alive."[21]

> A small shed had been added to my grandmother's house years ago. Some boards were laid across the joists at the top, and between these boards and the roof was a very small garret. . . . The garret was only nine feet long and seven feet wide. The highest part was three feet high, and sloped down abruptly to the loose board floor. There was no admission for either light or air. My uncle Phillip, who was a carpenter, had very skillfully made a concealed trap-door, which communicated with the storeroom. . . . To this hole I was conveyed as soon as I entered the house. The air was stifling; the darkness total. . . It was impossible for me to move in an erect position, but I crawled about my den for exercise. (*I* 114-15)

The configurations of the garret itself, as well as its (lack of) relation to the social space that lies "outside" it, work to code Brent's "(loop)hole" as a specifically uterine, maternal enclosure. Like the mythologized place of the bourgeois subject's gestation, the garret is airless and completely without light, sealed from the "exterior" by all but a single, and deftly concealed, connecting passage; moreover, Brent's existence in this sanctuary rearranges her body, forces her into the prone positions of the human infant. But more decisive for an understanding of the "loophole" as the zone of the white maternal origin, this enclosure is impossible to situate; rather, it represents the alterity, or "elsewhere," of any space we can delineate. Thus, for example, the garret is not "in" the slave state of North Carolina, since it is the condition of her existence as a slave that Brent refuses by turning fugitive. As Valerie Smith observes, by suggesting that her confinement was *preferable* to her lot as a slave, Jacobs effectively "dates her emancipation from the time she entered her loophole, even though she did not cross over into the free states until seven years later."[22] Neither, however, is the garret "in" the north, inasmuch as from her locus of retreat she simulates a flight—which, only by reason of its unreality, becomes impossible to check. Furthermore, the garret is deleted from the already marginal site of the grandmother's house, which as the legal property of an emancipated slave has functioned in the lives of Brent and her children as a kind of tenuous free zone: in order to allay suspicion, the grandmother proceeds to put Brent's absence on display, by contriving to give visitors the "complete" tour of her premises. The interiorized space of the garret remains conspicuously in excess of the socially and politically demarcatable terrains to which Brent has been or might be assigned.

For Brent to enter into the interiorized domain of white motherhood is *not* to render her motherhood representable. The point is repeatedly dramatized in the text, as the captive mourns her inability to signify her existence to her children.

> But I was not comfortless. I heard the voices of my children. There was joy and there was sadness in the sound. It made my tears flow. How I longed to speak to them! (*I* 114)

After she drills a small hole, "about an inch long and an inch broad," in the garret's wall, and gains visual access to the outside, Brent remains unable to articulate her presence to the children whom she now, however, freely monitors from her place of concealment.[23] Secreted in the zone of the original maternal body, she comes, paradoxically, to occupy the phantasmatic position of the voyeur, of the absolute presence who sees without subjecting herself to the other's gaze. As the distinction between the radical non-being of the muted subject and the absolute being of the invisible spectator is collapsed, both poles, or positions, are derealized.

> At last I heard the merry laugh of children, and presently two sweet little faces were looking up at me, as though they knew I was there, and were conscious of the joy they imparted. How I longed to *tell* them I was there! (*I* 115)

Season after season, year after year, I peeped at my children's faces, and heard their sweet voices, with a heart yearning all the while to say, "Your mother is here." (*I* 148)

Jacobs articulates the proposition "Your mother is here" in the guise of what must remain unspoken. In so doing, she simultaneously claims for Brent the unconditional identity of the naturalized mother, while exposing naturalized motherhood as an uninhabitable discourse for the decommodified female subject. The children gaze up, "as though they knew"—would always recognize their mother, no matter that she cannot make herself present to them. But, crucially, whereas both children do eventually learn of their mother's proximity, they aptly interpret her presence "here" to require her discursive erasure. Early in his mother's retreat, Benny hears a "cough up over the wood shed," which for no particular reason, as he acknowledges, "made me think it was you" (*I* 154); and, some years later, Brent slips into the house to risk a farewell with Ellen, about to depart in the service of the father who had since become master as well. Both children's precocious ability to remain mute, their recognition that the condition of their mother's continued presence is that it remain unspoken, functions in this portion of the narrative as the sign of their affective bond to her and, by extension, as the legitimation of her motherhood.[24]

In one sense, by maintaining silence about the mother's presence "here," the children validate Brent's motherhood within the conventional terms of sentimental discourse, where the maternal bond is coded as what can never be put into words. However, Brent's unrepresentability as naturalized maternal body converges with her unrepresentability as fugitive commodity, to expose naturalized motherhood as an abstraction and appropriation of the female body in another register—this time, in the register of (white) gender rather than that of (black) race. In other words, there are two distinct economies in which the phrase "Your mother is here" cannot be said: the sentimental economy, in which the mother inhabits the elsewhere of the origin (i.e., the mother is never really *here*); and the economy of slavery, in which motherhood is unintelligible as an affective social bond (i.e., that which is here is not really a *mother*). The children's silence signifies equally in both. It conforms to the logic of sentimental representation, in which the mother's love is ineffable, an affect in excess of discourse; at the same time, their silence must also be deciphered as a gesture of knowing complicity in the staging of the commodified mother's escape. By running together the discourses of the naturalized and the commodified maternal bodies in this way, Jacobs both effects the naturalization of the commodified body *and* points to the denaturalization of motherhood as *a further condition of the captive body's decommodification*—where decommodification is understood as the possibility of being there, of saying "Your mother is here."

If neither Brent nor her children can say where she is, she can nonetheless, from within the confines of the garret, signify her presence *as though from elsewhere*. Drafting a letter to Dr. Flint, she arranges to have the letter posted from the north, thus devising to speak to him as though she had eluded his search—significantly, she claims to be established in Massachusetts, one of the most secure havens for fugitives before passage of the Fugitive Slave Law. Confronted with the evidence of her successful flight, Flint seeks to forge an authority over Brent he no longer possesses. He produces a duplicate letter, in which Brent, rather than reproach him "the years of misery he had brought upon her" (*I* 128-29), implores instead his permission to return south. As he calls on Brent's grandmother with this proof of Brent's submission, he stumbles over Ellen in play next to the storeroom, and pauses to assure her: "'Yes, Ellen, I am going to bring [your mother] home very soon . . . and you shall see her as much as you like, you curly-headed nigger.' This was as good as comedy to me," Brent adds, "who had heard it all" (*I* 130). While Flint exposes to the (concealed) Brent the counterfeit nature of his mastery, Brent's simulated liberation acquires in Flint's mind the stamp of authenticity.

The fact that Dr. Flint had written to the mayor of Boston convinced me that he believed my letter to be genuine, and of course that he had no suspicion of my being anywhere in the vicinity. It was a great object to keep up this delusion, for it made me and my friends feel less anxious, and it would be very convenient whenever there was a chance to escape. I resolved therefore to continue to write letters from the north from time to time. (*I* 131-32)

Brent's letters to Dr. Flint resituate the zone of naturalized white motherhood in relation to the symbolic order: the garret becomes a strategic location for the staging of a fictional emancipation—an imagined accession to representable identity—that crucially enables her actual escape from commodity status. Inscribing herself within the dominant gender discourse of antebellum culture, in which the (white) mother is constituted as affecting absence, Jacobs brings the experience of radical commodification to bear on the gendered position she assumes. She retreats into the dark interior of the white maternal body only to demonstrate that this space is not fully within itself, to unravel the structuring binary interior/exterior and transform the politics of maternal love.

Postscript

Postmodern Subjectivity and Virtual Motherhood

Besides, although the creation of life *in vitro* would certainly be a scientific feat worthy of note—and probably even a Nobel Prize—it would not, in the long run, tell us much more about the space of *possible* life than we already know. [. . .] Computers should be thought of as an important laboratory tool for the study of life, substituting for the array of incubators, culture dishes, microscopes, electrophoretic gels, pipettes, centrifuges and other assorted wet-lab paraphernalia, one simple to master piece of experimental equipment devoted exclusively to *the incubation of information structures.* (Final emphasis added)
— Chris Langton

Motherhood acts as a limit to the conceptualization of femininity as a scientific construction of mechanical and electrical parts. And yet it is also that which infuses the machine with the breath of a human spirit. The maternal and the mechanical/synthetic coexist in a relation that is a curious imbrication of dependence and antagonism.
— Mary Ann Doane

If your woman is a ghost, she doesn't know it. Neither will you.
— Neuromancer to Case

This postscript is concerned with the imbrication, to borrow Mary Ann Doane's term,[1] of ideologically incommensurate discourses: it examines the ostensibly unthinkable affinities between synthetic or simulated bodies and naturalized identities, between artificial reproduction and the fetishized maternal body, between the cybernetic womb and a phantasmatics of origins. I am interested in the way that contemporary reproductive discourse perpetuates the essentialized construction of motherhood that it apparently supplants, both metaphorically ("the incubation of information structures")[2] and materially (by maintaining the historical invisibility of the mother before the law, for example). Here I am particularly concerned to explore how cyberpunk as a genre, and *Neuromancer* as one its defining texts, functions like the discourse of reproductive technology to reinscribe nature on the maternal body. As a result, *Neuromancer* preserves a specifically humanist logic of embodiment, (pre-) oedipality and gendered subjectivity, that it appears so ostentatiously to undo.

In other words, I want to trace the limits of cyberpunk's posthumanism, if only to qualify the typically and prematurely celebratory inflection of its theorists' claims. For instance, Veronica Hollinger affirms that ". . . in its representation of 'monsters'— hopeful or otherwise—produced by the interface of the human and the machine, [cyberpunk] *radically decenters the human body,* the sacred icon of the essential self, in the same way that the virtual reality of cyberspace works to decenter the conventional humanist notions of an unproblematical 'real.'"[3] More particularly, I wish to destabilize the terms of Joan Gordon's rather facile distinction between the nostalgic organicism of "overtly" feminist science fiction and the more usefully, if only implicitly feminist, post-organicism of cyberpunk. Indeed, she argues:

> Virtually every feminist SF utopia dreams of a pastoral world, fueled by organic structures rather than mechanical ones, inspired by versions of the archetypal Great Mother. And virtually every feminist SF novel, utopian or not, incorporates a longing to go forward into the idealized

past of earth's earlier matriarchal nature religions. Because cyberpunk extrapolates from the 1980's—not a sterling time for feminism in the world at large—it's no wonder few women are presently involved in the movement. Nevertheless, cyberpunk does much that could enrich overt feminist SF *by directing it away from nostalgia.* . . . Feminist SF consistently avoids the kind of intrusive technology cyberpunk embraces.[4]

In many respects, Gordon's argument is compelling: her claim that the temporality of this utopianism is dangerous for feminism, that it brackets a relation to history as a field of multiple contingencies and possibilities, is persuasive. So, too, is her corollary, that cyberpunk's representation of the human body as a denatured phenomenon opens up the body's relation to history and technology in ways that are productive for feminism. Still, Gordon too readily perceives in cyberpunk's post-organicism the demise of a utopianism she associates here all too narrowly and conveniently with feminist SF. Thus, Gordon assumes, because cyberpunk repudiates the organicist aesthetic of "overtly" feminist science fiction, its own temporality is necessarily progressive, its texts necessarily resistant to historical and corporeal closure. Because organicism turns on the nostalgia for origins, however, it does not follow that this nostalgia, and the sentimental narratives it structures, are always and exclusively organicist. On the contrary, I will argue that *Neuromancer's* technophilia elaborates precisely its nostalgia for an idealized matriarchal past; Gibson's cyberpunk sensibility is constituted in loss and rendered in the impossible tense of a perpetual return to an originary site of restitution.

Therefore, I contend with Mary Ann Doane that technology and the maternal "coexist" in an impossibly doubled relation, occupying at once discontinuous and contingent domains. On one level, the maternal body defined as the site of natural reproduction traces the outer boundary to the field of technological reproduction. Still, technologies of reproduction, such as film (or, I would add, technologies of simulation such as cyberspace), assume the existence of something prior to themselves, of an original or material object; insofar as the technological reproduction of this original at once effects and disavows its loss, Doane suggests, technology recapitulates the relation of the fetishist to the maternal body. Commenting on Christian Metz's notion of the "cinema fetishist," a subject whose enjoyment of film hinges on an appreciation both of the presence on which the cinematic image trades and of the absence that subtends it, Doane observes: "Technological fetishism, through its alliance of technology with a process of concealing and revealing lack, is theoretically returned to the body of the mother . . . theory understands the obsession with technology as a tension of movement toward and away from the mother."[5]

If technologies of reproduction thus reproduce the logic of the fetishist's desire, so too, and in more contradictory fashion, do reproductive technologies—the very technologies that appear to dislodge the mother from the privileged position she occupies in the fetishist's psychic economy. In the freudian determination of this economy, that which the fetishist simultaneously affirms and refuses is the loss of the phallic mother, of the maternal body as figure of originary plenitude. Yet it is exactly the status of the maternal body as origin that the substitution of an artificial reproductive apparatus would seem to endanger. By enabling us to reproduce the maternal body, to fertilize the egg, and, hypothetically at least, to incubate the fetus in a fully synthetic environment, reproductive technologies appear to propel the fetishist and his fundamentally nostalgic desire into a simulated world, without origin and without end, to wrench him from the sentimental and insert him into a postmodern narrative frame. Doane's analysis, however, allows us to see how reproductive technologies might participate in the naturalizing discourse of motherhood that they ostensibly disrupt; how on the simulated womb that we expect to encounter somewhere altogether beyond the logic of the nature/technology binary, we can nevertheless discern a fetishization of the maternal body.

Ectogenesis in the Nineteenth Century

In an article for *Hypatia's* special issue on ethics and reproduction, Julien Murphy struggles to delineate a feminist position
on ectogenesis, or *in vitro* gestation.

> Clearly, many feminists would favor pregnancy over IVG in most cases,
> not because women are the most cost-effective uteri . . . but because IVG
> represents a misguided approach to infertility. That some women might
> prefer gestation of their fertilized eggs in a laboratory rather than in their
> own bodies is more a mark of the oppressive ways in which women's
> bodies and pregnancy are constructed in this culture rather than a sign
> of progressive social attitudes.[6]

Feminists should reject this form of liberation from the female
body, Murphy concludes; the technology of IVG only appeals to
women in the context of our culture's devaluation of pregnancy as
a physical limitation and an economic liability, a devaluation
which a feminist politics should aim to contest rather than cir-
cumvent. Yet, as Valerie Hartouni has recently shown, the discourse of IVG functions *not* to emancipate women from the
marked female body, but, quite the contrary, to *return* the "emancipated," white, professional woman to her ("natural") body.
Patrick Steptoe, a fertility expert and engineer of the first so-called
"test-tube baby," puts it this way: "It is a fact that there is a biological drive to reproduce. Women who deny this drive, or in whom
it is frustrated, show disturbances in other ways."[7] Thus, Hartouni
reminds us, reproductive technology legitimates its intervention in
female reproduction by claiming to "help women realize their maternal nature, their innate need to mother."[8] Moreover, while this
high-cost technology thereby reinscribes "women" in "nature"
(from which Murphy projects them as freed), "nature" remains a
race- and class-bound category. By omitting to consider who is tar-
geted by this technology,[9] Murphy elides what Hartouni identifies
as "both [the] text and subtext" of fertility research: "[W]hite
women want babies but cannot have them, and black and other

'minority' women, coded as 'breeders' within American society (and welfare dependents within Reagan's America) are having babies 'they' cannot take care of and 'we' do not want."[10] A feminist analysis of this reproductive technology, then, needs to acknowledge that ectogenesis was developed specifically to enhance the reproductive capacity of white middle-class women; furthermore, whereas ectogenesis displaces reproduction from these women's bodies, the discourse of ectogenesis (conversely) serves to essentialize their relation to their culturally constructed reproductive function—to motherhood.

In documenting both the "pronatalist" and the racist agendas that underwrite contemporary reproductive technologies, Hartouni corroborates but also crucially contextualizes Doane's argument, assigning a race and a class to Doane's techno-fetishized maternal body: to align the politics of the fertility clinic with the phantasmatics of technophilia and visual pleasure[11] is (among other things) to begin to locate the pre-oedipal (or phallic) mother within historically contingent social formations of race and class, as well as gender. Before unfolding the pertinence of ectogenesis to *Neuromancer*, then, I want to place the technological fetishism it exemplifies more fully in relation to the historical constitution of the white maternal body, in order at once to account for the cultural dominance of the (techno-) fetishist's desire, and to avoid the risk of essentializing his desire that Doane's analysis incurs. Indeed, Doane's model arguably moves us away from a totalizing discourse on motherhood, in which the natural maternal body is essentialized as origin, into a totalizing discourse on discursivity, in which the simulated maternal body is essentialized as a structure of desire. Thus we need also to situate the fetishist's desire with respect to a particular class of historical subjects, and thereby to delimit fetishism's cultural logic—to represent it as *a* cultural logic, rather than *the* logic of technology and technological reproduction. If adequately historicized as a product of a liberal bourgeois order, Doane's model productively engages the material difficulties of dismantling that order, difficulties that cyberpunk's theorists are prone to slight. The point is to acknowledge the centrality of the fetishist's ambivalence to the bourgeois subject and the freudian narrative of subject formation,[12] while bearing in mind that this formation is neither necessary, nor universal, nor by any means uncontested.[13]

I have argued that a particular narrative of motherhood emerges, with the middle-class nuclear family, in the late eighteenth and early nineteenth centuries. In this narrative, motherhood is constructed as a rationalized natural function, subordinate to the logic of a liberal political order, even as it places the woman in the impossible beyond of language, signification, and social being. In the psychoanalytic mapping of this bourgeois family, to enter into the symbolic order, to become a subject, is precisely to separate from the mother. The acquisition of identity, in all its permutations, is seen as contingent on the founding loss of the maternal body, for which the henceforth generalized nostalgia is also inevitably laced with the horror of self-annihilation. Thus the organization of the fetishist's desire—his signature irresolution with respect to the maternal body, his movement toward and away from the mother— reappears at the level of the constitution of the freudian subject as such. Most notably, of course, in the discussion of the fort/da game, and in the strangely circular notion of progress that characterizes *Beyond the Pleasure Principle* as a whole,[14] Freud discovers the fetishist's doubled trajectory in the motions of every mother's son. The ambivalent relation to the maternal that structures "fetishism," conceived as a particular form or "pathology" of desire, may be seen to structure the bourgeois subject at large, along a slightly different, though finally convergent, axis—with reference to a lack of, rather than in, the mother's body. In this sense, fetishism represents a cultural logic of identity, the *mise en jeu* of the subject's own loss—or rather, of the freudian subject *as* loss.

Remarkably, moreover, from the bourgeois mother's standpoint, motherhood entails a kind of symbolic ectogenesis that prefigures, and arguably informs, its technological literalization: inasmuch as the maternal body is constructed as exterior to language and sociality, motherhood transpires in excess of (prior to) any and all social and discursive determinations of the mother's body. To figure the ("biological") essence of motherhood as something ahistorical and unspeakable is to render it external to any incarnation of motherhood, to any particular female subject. The mother is one place as a socially and symbolically apprehended and apprehensible entity, but elsewhere—outside of herself—in the performance of her reproductive function.

While the technology of ectogenesis resituates the "essence" of motherhood, renders it all too accessible to the regulatory apparatus of the scientific gaze, the division it appears to engender in the figure of the essential mother is in fact a division constitutive of bourgeois motherhood. In this frame, it becomes possible to understand two central attributes of *Neuromancer*'s plot: first, motherhood occurs outside the body of the mother in the artificial "matrix" known as cyberspace; second, this exteriority only confirms the mother's privileged status as the object of filial yearning and terror. In its representation of reproduction, then, *Neuromancer* reinscribes a specifically bourgeois logic of identity on the postmodern technoworld of hybridized and augmented bodies. However, reinscription implies slippage as well as continuity; even as it preserves this middle-class formation, *Neuromancer* suggests how essential motherhood might be contested in a postmodern register, through the text's imagined alteration of the working-class woman's body. The final section of my essay will consider how Gibson's romance of the techno-fetishized mother interrupts itself at the site of Molly's "working girl" technobody, in and on which a competing discourse of motherhood emerges—one I distinguish as "polychromatic," borrowing Donna Haraway's term.[15]

Birth in the Corporate Data Bank

Most obviously, of course, Gibson's cyberspace represents the negation of embodiment, and hence of procreation, motherhood, and other embodied functions; it is, in Gibson's famous formulation, a "consensual hallucination," "a graphic representation of data abstracted from the banks of every computer in the human system."[16] Cyberspace is "lines of light ranged in the nonspace of the mind, clusters and constellations of data," a space defined by the impossibility of *being there* at all. To "jack in" to cyberspace is to jettison "the meat," the flesh conceived as an impediment to pleasure. Debarred from cyberspace as punishment for cheating his employers, Case experiences his return to the body as a kind of psychical amputation.

> They damaged his nervous system with a wartime Russian mycotoxin.
> Strapped to the bed in a Memphis hotel, his talent burning out micron by micron, he hallucinated for thirty hours.
> The damage was minute, subtle and utterly effective.
> For Case, who'd lived for the bodiless exultation of cyberspace, it was the Fall. The body was meat. Case fell into the prison of his own flesh. (*N* 6)

Considering the vulnerability of the masculine body in the techno-culture of cyberpunk, where that body depends on "prosthetic help," and on "the reconstructive aid of a whole range of genetic overhauls and cybernetic enhancements," Andrew Ross has characterized cyberpunk masculinity as embattled. "These enhancements and retrofits were technotoys the boys always dreamed of having, but they were also body-altering and castrating in ways that boys always had nightmares about. [. . .] Such a body would be a battleground in itself, where traditional male 'resistance' to domination was uneasily coopted by the cutting-edge logic of new capitalist technologies."[17] Newly permeable, penetrated by the intrusive technologies that render him socially functional, the cyberpunk male interfaces with the corporate world at the price of his corporeal integrity. Yet Case's contempt for the body as "meat," in this passage and elsewhere, suggests a distinction between the gendering of the techno-body, defined by its capacity to enter into the network, or informational matrix, to penetrate the corporate body, and the gendering of the flesh, the colonized organic matter, which is made to bear the stigma of the violations it undergoes. The feminization of the techno-body, in other words, is displaced onto its organic component, and disavowed at the site of its technological enhancements. What Case experiences as castrating is not the openness of his feminized body to technology, but the loss of his "technotoys," of his ability to "jack in."[18]

For Case to access cyberspace is to cancel the lack in and of the feminized flesh: while cyberspace represents the loss of all the material world, at the level of technologically simulated experience it effects a negation of all loss. Cyberspace offers nothing less to the intrepid cowboy than "limitless subjective dimensions," that "unfold" before him in a "fluid neon origami trick," to form a "transparent 3D chessboard extending to infinity" (N 52). In this sense, Gibson's paradigmatic cyberpunk novel concerns less the masculine body (and less still its rescripting), than the masculine subject's relation to the maternal body as the imagined locus of an original plenitude. Jacking into cyberspace, the cowboy both assures that the maternal/matter will be lacking and disavows his loss of the mother's body—this loss in which his own delimited and contingent subjectivity is founded. So it is that the artificial intelligence named Wintermute can terrorize a newly restored and cyberspace-happy Case with the image of a prolific womb, which to the fully posthuman subject should simply fail to matter—in this instance, with a cracked-open wasps' nest Case once observed.

> He saw the thing the shell of gray paper had concealed. Horror. The spiral birth factory, stepped terraces of the hatching cells, blind jaws of the unborn moving ceaselessly, the staged progress from egg to larva, near-wasp, wasp. In his mind's eye, a kind of time-lapse photography took place, revealing the thing as the biological equivalent of a machine gun. Hideous in its perfection. Alien. (N 126)

At any rate, for Case, who incinerates the nest in panic just as Wintermute hopes he will destroy whatever attaches to this image, cyberspace signifies, not the reconfiguration of phallic masculinity, but the fetishization of the maternal.

Of course, what attaches to the hive is the corporate entity known as Tessier-Ashpool, which owns both Wintermute and another AI, known as Neuromancer. Characterized in the novel as an "atavism," an organization structured like a "clan" rather than a multinational, Tessier-Ashpool shows itself in the course of the novel to be at once provisional and specifically matriarchal in form. Provisional, insofar as the clan matriarch, Marie-France Tessier, gestates in the corporation's cybernetic hive of data an artificial life, whose birth at the novel's conclusion both eternalizes herself as origin and imposes a utopian teleology on cyberspace. Literally, this denouement involves the (re)birth or fusion of the two AIs Neuromancer and Wintermute into a single, self-conscious mind, into the self-consciousness of the cyberspace matrix itself. Pursuing Wintermute's own metaphor, however, Case figures this outcome as the hatching of a new life from the cybernetic nest.

> [Case] stared down . . . remembering his flash of comprehension as the Kuang program had penetrated the ice beneath the towers, his single glimpse of the structure of information 3Jane's dead mother had evolved there. He'd understood then why Wintermute had chosen the nest to represent it, but he'd felt no revulsion. She'd seen through the sham immortality of cryogenics; unlike Ashpool and their other children—aside from 3Jane—she'd refused to stretch her time into a series of warm blinks strung along a chain of winter.
>
> Wintermute was hive mind, decision maker, effecting change in the world outside. Neuromancer was personality. Neuromancer was immortality. Marie-France must have built something into Wintermute, the compulsion that had driven the thing to free itself, to unite with Neuromancer. (N 269)

Marie-France's "incubation of information structures," to borrow Langton's term, indicates not only her dissatisfaction with suspended animation as a means to immortality, but the inadequacy of genetic replication, or cloning, as well. In the replication of serial offspring, the "mother" figures as no more than a genetic code. Cloning demystifies motherhood by reducing the mother to a data string, rendering irrelevant the disposition of her body. (By contrast, ectogenesis, signifying literally "exterior generation," necessarily engages the *relation* between the gestating child and the body from which it has been externalized, or displaced.) Marie-France desires continuity, the affirmation of her essence, and secures it through her appropriation of the corporate data bank for the gestation of simulated life—in her ectogenesis of cyberspace as living entity. In the rather elliptically rendered account of the two AIs (re)birth as one, Gibson nonetheless discloses at the novel's end the affiliation of cyberspace to the maternal and the discourse of origins.

Case's revulsion at the image of the teeming wasps' nest vanishes at the spectacle of its artificial analog; in the contemplation of this simulated womb, the fetishist's desire completes its impossibly doubled trajectory toward and away from his origins. The data nest is both vacuous—its contents have no actual existence—and replete with the life of the matrix itself. With *Neuromancer,* I propose, we are back in the logic of the sentimental novel—where what is excessive is maternal but what is maternal is never finally in excess. Moreover, the novel prospectively extends the structure of Case's desire to a rather unusual subject—to the fully inorganic and incorporeal life form Marie-France has mothered. Although bound in a literal sense to the matrix of his creation—having, after all become the matrix—the new-born Wintermute/Neuromancer begins to know himself as partial, to look away, like any properly socialized boy, from the dark scene of his origin and toward the world beyond. In their parting conversation, Case inquires,

"So what are you."
"I'm the matrix, Case."
Case laughed. "Where's that get you?"
"Nowhere. Everywhere. I'm the sum total of the works. The whole show." [. . .]

"But what do you do? You just *there?*"
"I talk to my own kind."
"But you're the whole thing. Talk to yourself?"
"There's others. I found one already. Series of transmissions recorded over a period of eight years, in the 1970's. 'Til there was me, natch, there was nobody to know, nobody to answer."
"From where?"
"Centauri system."
"Oh," Case said. "Yeah? No shit?"
"No shit."
And then the screen went blank. (*N* 269-70)

Wintermute/Neuromancer thus asserts the plenitude of his existence at the very moment that his entry into intersubjectivity requires an acknowledgment of his partiality; inasmuch as there are "others," the matrix is not "the whole show." The scenario of loss and disavowal, audible in this artificial life form's rather hilariously human aspiration to the "limitless subjective dimensions" for which the human cowboy hankers, suggests at the very least that the desire for integrity is not merely, or conveniently, restricted to an explicitly organic frame of reference.

Beyond Fetishism

Case's successful accessing of the Tessier-Ashpool corporate information bank, his achievement of techno-masculine functionality, rejoins the conventional narrative development of the masculine subject, as the ostensibly posthuman dialectic of the cowboy-computer interface yields to Case's contemplation of the fetishized data "nest." Against this reduction, it is worth examining the alternate view of and into the Tessier-Ashpool corporate body that the narrative provides, a view as plainly associated with Neuromancer's personality, and hence with Marie-France herself, as the metaphor of the nest was aligned with Wintermute. In fact, the crucial difference between the two AIs conception of the Tessier-Ashpool corporate space may already be discerned in Wintermute's recourse to metaphor: in figuring the data bank as nest, Wintermute at once brings the virtual home to the maternal, and preserves the distance between them, thus sustaining the gap in which the techno-fetishist installs himself. Wintermute's figure, like Case's disavowal of the mother's loss, turns on the simultaneous identity and non-identity of the maternal body and the virtual womb, which is at once lacking with respect to the flesh (not "really" there) and the very essence of embodied motherhood. In Neuromancer's signifying economy, however, the space mapped in and by Wintermute's figure vanishes, as a non-binary alterity interrupts this mirror play of identity and difference.

Neuromancer's attempt to communicate with Case involves the cowboy's wrenching dislocation, from the nowhere/everywhere of the computer matrix to the elsewhere of the "rim," the border, where Case, whose heart has (literally) ceased to beat—who has, in the cowboys' graphic idiom, "flatlined"—effectively outlives himself—lives beyond any determination of his selfhood to which either being or non-being might be ascribed.

> Nothing. Gray void.
> No matrix, no grid. No cyberspace.
> The deck was gone. His fingers were. . . .
> And on the far rim of consciousness, a scurrying, a fleeting impression of something rushing toward him, across leagues of black mirror.
> He tried to scream. (N 233)

The trajectory of the masculine subject, toward the outer limit of the knowable, is here reversed, as Case, suspended in the void, perceives the limit attaining *him*—in an inversion of the romance paradigm that (with a remarkable economy of prose) throws Western epistemology into crisis. In Neuromancer's "black mirror," the interminable doubling and negation of the body ceases:[19] while Case awakens from this implosion of his consciousness to find himself "crouched" in the fetal position, "his arms wrapped tight across his knees," on the wet sand of an ocean beach, this posture is here displaced from the origin story in which it is conventionally inscribed. Case is returned, not to the mother's body, but to his own; his crouching form is conspicuous, not for its integrity, its seamless connection to the (m)other, but for its partiality, its incomplete delineation, signalled by Case's imperfect control of his excretions. Moreover, Case is not "returned" at all, insofar as a return is always figurative, but rather enters into a simulated reality fully as material as the "meat" Case reviles:

> Sand stung his cheek. He put his face against his knees and wept, the sound of his sobbing as distant and alien as the cry of the searching gull. Hot urine soaked his jeans, dribbled on the sand, and quickly cooled in the wind off the water. When his tears were gone, his throat ached. . . .
>
> His knees and elbows ached. His nose was running; he wiped it on the cuff of his jacket, then searched one empty pocket after another. "Jesus," he said, shoulders hunched, tucking his fingers beneath his arms for warmth. (N 233-34)

Neuromancer's otherworld neither figures nor (consequently) transcends the flesh; rather, Case discovers, Neuromancer reconfigures (recomputes) the material world, and so too, we must surmise, the body Case acquires here, within a different symbolic register, as a series of "number[s] coded in a mathematical system that existed nowhere outside the mind of Neuromancer" (N 258). This computer simulation demands interrogation, less in itself—the seascape Neuromancer fabricates for Case is vaguely horrifying in its non-linear temporality, the looming absence of histories or futures—than for the categories of knowledge it functions to disrupt. Thus when Case encounters his dead girlfriend living in a bunker on the beach, he finds that Linda Lee subtly strays from between the poles of abysmal presence and fetishized lack that had previously served to structure his relation to her body. She is no longer simply the "meat," her paint-smudged eyes those of "some animal pinned in the headlights of an oncoming vehicle" (N 8), nor the fetish, excessive in the very fact of her social dysfunction, of her pathetically inept imposture of a streetsmart hustler. At first Case continues to alternate between a construction of Linda as phantom—"you aren't anything," he informs her—and as techno-fetish, her computer-generated flesh bringing Case back to some "vast thing, *beyond knowing,* a sea of information coded in spiral and pheromone, infinite intricacy, that only the body, in its strong blind way, could ever read" (*N* 239, emphasis added). But the possibility of disavowing the loss of this "vast thing" that belongs, as Case remembers, to the "meat," is finally undercut by the impossibility of *knowing* it to be lost, when reality is an enumeration, a number series on a memory chip, in which presence and absence alike have become unthinkable.[20] Appearing on the beach in the form of a laughing, brown boy, Neuromancer gives voice to the fetishist's impasse.

> "Neuromancer," the boy said, slitting long gray eyes against the rising sun. "The lane to the land of the dead. Where you are, my friend. Marie-France, my lady, she prepared this road, but her lord choked her off before I could read the book of her days. Neuro from the nerves, the silver paths. Romancer. Necromancer. I call up the dead. But no, my friend," and the boy did a little dance, brown feet printing the sand, "I am the dead, and their land." He laughed. A gull cried, "Stay. If your woman is a ghost, she doesn't know it. Neither will you." (*N* 243-44)

Case cannot disavow what he cannot also affirm; and he cannot know whether Neuromancer's dead are ghosts, only that their non/existence is determinate—infuriatingly so. "I don't know," he concedes to Linda, as he hands her his jacket in tacit refusal of her plea that he stay, "maybe you're here. Anyway, it gets cold" (*N* 244).

Of course, it is not without resonance for Case's terse refusal that this alternative conception of cyberspace derives from the "other," Rio-based AI. (Wintermute, by contrast, is a Swiss citizen.) That Neuromancer, often simply identified in the novel by place name, as "Rio," fashions his icon after a beach-combing Brazilian boy is at best ironic, inasmuch as brown third world children rarely have access to global data networks, while in their material and ideological operations, succinctly characterized by Donna Haraway as an "informatics of domination," such networks might nonetheless delimit these children's lives.[21] More perniciously, insofar as "Rio" is the product of a Western woman's programming, the AI's icon must be decoded with and against the history of orientalism—so that Marie-France's reconceptualization of cyberspace, via Neuromancer, as a non-reflective mirror is launched, perversely, under the sign of the appropriated other. Still, Neuromancer's mocking brown boy icon remains also obliquely suggestive of the possibility that cyberspace could be discontinuous and multiple, cyberspaces, in which radically contestatory narratives of social reality might be rendered.

Polychromatic Motherhood

If Neuromancer suggests how the multiplication and diversification of agencies might disjoin the "matrix," and thereby inhibit the installation of cyberspace as a totalized informational "grid," the figure of Molly points in complementary fashion to the ways in which cybernetic alterations and enhancements of the embodied subject function to rescript Enlightenment constructions of identity. Donna Haraway has emerged as a primary theorist of such cyborg subjectivities and indeed it is with reference to her encoding of the term that I designate Molly as a "polychromatic" mother.

> [My cyborg] is a polychromatic girl . . . the cyborg is a bad girl, she is really not a boy. Maybe she is not so much bad as she is a shape-changer, whose dislocations are never free. She is a girl who's trying not to become Woman, but remain responsible to women of many colors and positions, and who hasn't really figured out a politics that makes the necessary articulations with the boys who are your allies. It's undone work.[22]

Given this elaboration of the concept, it is arguably impossible, or at any rate counterproductive, to translate the girl into a mother;

the dislocation of her essence that I earlier proposed was constitutive of the essentialized mother—a dislocation that effects the transformation of a particular class of women into "Woman"—would seem to preempt and recontain the cyborg girl's defining capacity for multiple and self-conscious dislocations. However, Molly is precisely *not* a mother, but a "girl" modified to simulate the maternal, a cyborg who shape-shifts into a mother, in a temporary dislocation that constitutes a narrative of non-original motherhood.[23] To be sure, dislocations are never without a price, neither for the shifter, nor for those whom her dislocations displace: Molly's techno-simulation of the maternal here is crucial, since she produces for Case a field of disturbance from which he cannot so easily jack out.

Molly's technological modifications function to dislocate her across a series of boundaries, of which the organic/cybernetic is only the most apparent. Her permanent alterations include surgically inset lenses, "sealing her sockets . . . [so that the] lenses seemed to grow from smooth pale skin above her cheekbones" (*N* 24) and retractable, four-centimeter scalpel blades implanted under her (burgundy) nails. These alterations position her on the boundary of the human and the animal as well as the human and the machine; moreover, Molly's cybernetic modifications, while first refigured in the narrative as animal attributes, are then refigured anew as maternal, thereby placing her—in a striking reorganization of established binaries—at the limit of the maternal and the organic-human. Thus Molly's blank lenses are said to examine Case "with an insect calm" (*N* 30), while later in the narrative their "empty quicksilver" surface serves as the mirror in which a "fetal" Case discerns his (interestingly) perfected form (*N* 256). Her augmented nails inspire feline metaphors, most notably on the part of the "Panther Moderns," an urban street gang with whom Molly finds herself teamed on a raid, and who adopt her as "Cat Mother" of their "Brood" (*N* 64). The Moderns' ready incorporation of Molly into their subculture further maps her slippage across boundaries of gender and (more obscurely) race, insofar as they are apparently all-male and (more ambiguously) non-white. (The snapshot of an exemplary Modern initially strikes Case not as a singular entity, but "a collage of some kind"; elsewhere, the Moderns' "nihilistic technofetishism" is exemplified more particularly in a "soft-voiced boy called Angelo," whose skingrafts and implanted canines give him the "smooth and hideous" appearance of a shark [*N* 58-59].) If Molly's "articulations with the boys who are [her] allies" are "undone work," her provisional status as cyborg cat mother to this adolescent male brood nonetheless indicates the multiple junctures at which such articulations might occur.

Crucially, this "working girl's" alliances are professional, not political (*N* 30). Molly begins by hiring herself out as a "meat puppet," to pay for her modifications, working as a high-tech prostitute, in whom the house implants a "cut-out chip," so that, in Molly's phrasing, "[she isn't] in," when "the goods" are up for "rent" (*N* 147). She then moves to hiring out as "street samurai" (*N* 30) or professional ninja, not incidentally to a similar class of privileged white males as formerly constituted her clientele. But this more recent line of work is also Molly's "game" (*N* 267), in which she flaunts and parodies a variety of hardboiled masculine styles, performing, as Case observes, "every bad-ass hero," he grew up on, "Sony Mao in the old Shaw videos, Mickey Chiba, the whole lineage back to Lee and Eastwood" (*N* 213). Molly's self-commodification, then, may be read as a form of politically charged self-authorship.[24] And it is under the rubric of "her game," so conceived, that I want to locate Molly's techno-miming of maternity for her business and sexual partner Case: in order for Case to key his cyberspace raid on the Tessier-Ashpool nest to Molly's actual break-in at the family compound, she is "fitted for a broadcast rig" (*N* 53) or "simstim" unit, that allows Case to access Molly's sensorium, to "flip" from cyberspace to her interior.

Suspicious of simstim as "basically a meat toy" (*N* 55), Case now finds himself "a rider," an excrescence on or more exactly in Molly's body. It is worth underscoring that the sensory-audio link is "one-way," that Case loses both motor capacity and speech.

Then he keyed the new switch.

    The abrupt jolt into other flesh. Matrix gone, a wave of sound and color. . . . She was moving through a crowded street, past stalls vending discount software, prices feltpenned on sheets of plastic, fragments of music from countless speakers. Smells of urine, free monomers, perfume, patties of frying krill. For a few frightened seconds he fought helplessly to control her body. Then he willed himself into passivity, became the passenger behind her eyes.

    The glasses didn't seem to cut down the sunlight at all. He wondered if the built-in amps compensated automatically. Blue alphanumerics winked the time, low in her left peripheral field. Showing off, he thought. (*N* 56)

In this rescripting of the originary mother/infant symbiosis as a contingent, technologically-mediated relation, several defining elements of subject formation in the ("natural") nuclear family are recast. First, motherhood becomes performative, an assumed, rather than a given, function; even viewed from the inside, the maternal body is unnatural—seamed, stylized, "built-in" and on. Significantly, however, Molly's flesh is not dominated, or subsumed, by the cybernetic, so that the life of the "meat," the smell of urine or frying grease, interfaces (or is it intra-faces?) with the winking alphanumerics. If ectogenesis involves the mother's technological projection into the antiseptic elsewhere of the cybernetic womb, performative motherhood entails the refashioning of the body itself, as the always makeshift (improvised, rigged) intersection of cybernetic and organic modalities. Second, rather than encounter her body elsewhere, out of language and out of time, this techno-mother inhabits it, as a socially situated subject, a "working girl." Thus displaced from the phantasmatic locus of the subject's prehistory, the maternal body ceases to be figurable as choric enclosure, becoming instead a partial container, interrupted and disjoined at the sites of its multiple articulations with the world.

    In this frame, the techno-fetishizing of the maternal is made impossible: neither originary (organic) plenitude, nor symbolic lack, the maternal body can no longer be constituted in and as its perpetual migration between these poles. The fetishist's movement is checked as the shape of the mother's difference is redrawn; it is no longer castration that she lays at the masculine subject's door, no more a singular lack, but rather lacks, shifting contingencies and subjective gaps. Contemplating the masculine body in the mirror of Molly's lenses (a mirror he has accessed, of course, internally, from the "dark" side), Case is confronted, not with a double in whom his own originary loss is disavowed, but with a radically discontinuous entity.

> He flipped.
> And found himself staring down, through Molly's one good eye, at a white-faced, wasted figure, afloat in a loose fetal crouch, a cyberspace deck between its thighs, a band of silver trodes above closed, shadowed eyes. The man's cheeks were hollowed with a day's growth of dark beard, his face slick with sweat.
> He was looking at himself. (N 255-56)

Here a blinded Case (eyes sealed closed) sees himself "seeing" himself (through the medium of an appended organ, of his "silver trodes") from the elsewhere of the mother's body—an elsewhere he inhabits, for the moment at any rate, as fully, or as partially, as his "own" flesh.[25] In this dizzying arrangement, the masculine body comes undone—becomes "undone work"—by being made to occupy the locus of its own (un)doing, the boundary between ungendered infant and engendered techno-subject. More accurately, this liminal body cuts two ways. One might read the cyberspace deck between "its" thighs as cybernetic fetish object; but perhaps, through this dislocation of the phallus, cyberspace comes home to the embodied subject, as a mark of internal differences?

Notes

Preface

1. Jameson, *Postmodernism,* 6.
2. In this sense, the black maternal body possesses what Carolyn Dinshaw calls "the touch of the queer" ("The Touch of the Queer," unpublished paper). In an attempt to think queerness transhistorically, Dinshaw defines this "touch" as that which operates in any particular historical moment or cultural site to denaturalize normative gender relations. Specifically, she proposes, the queer is to gender what woman is to patriarchy and the racial hybrid is to race. These critical analogies suggest the limits of thinking queerness as this kind of default category (all that is not normative gender), which begs the question of gender itself. That is, in order to think such concepts as "patriarchy," "gender," or "race," we need precisely to unravel the structure of this analogy; to ask (for instance) what the queer is to race, or the racial hybrid to gender.

1. The Limits of Liberal Discourse

1. See Kerber, *Women of the Republic,* especially 3–32.
2. Although the founders disenfranchise free white women in general, without particular reference to class, the "republican woman," as I emphasize here, emerges from the middle classes. The "republican woman" appears in the context of the newly privatized nuclear family, where her functions are defined as reproductive (bearing new citizens) and pedagogical. Thus she belongs neither to the pre-industrial home economy nor to the (industrial) working classes, but to the bourgeois "domestic sphere."
3. I admit here to a certain slippage in my use of the terms "republican" and "(liberal) democratic," which may be seen to represent two distinct political traditions. As Chantal Mouffe notes, for example, in a recent discussion of

radical feminist politics, the liberal tradition turns on the bourgeois public/private distinction in ways that the older republican tradition does not: "The distinction between public/private, central as it was for the assertion of individual liberty, acted therefore as a powerful principle of exclusion. Through the identification between the private and the domestic, it played indeed an important role in the subordination of women. Recently, several feminists and other critics of liberalism have been looking to the civic republican tradition for a different, more active conception of citizenship that emphasizes the value of political participation and *the notion of a common good, prior to and independent of individual desires and interests.*" Mouffe, "Feminism and Radical Politics," 377.

But the national or "common good," as articulated in early republican culture, is the "good" of a specific white masculine mercantile class, elevated to the status of a universal. My interest here is in the way that democratic principles of representation in the early republic render certain class interests unintelligible in a national context.

4. Spillers, "Mama's Baby, Papa's Maybe," 67.

5. Kerber rightly emphasizes the degree to which "Republican Motherhood" represents a woman's discourse on womanhood. But it is nevertheless a discourse engendered by the logic of democratic representation, as it emerges from the Founding Fathers' texts. "Republican Motherhood" (or, as I tend to call it, sentimental motherhood, by association with the literary and cultural genre that constitutes its most complex elaboration) becomes a woman's discourse as metadiscourse—one which reflects on the conditions of its own production, and thus functions potentially to denaturalize contingent historical formations.

6. Butler, *Gender Trouble*, 6–7.

7. Thus the *opposition* Chantal Mouffe sets up between the study of historically constituted identities on the one hand, and the construction of transformed and transforming political subjectivities on the other, seems to me questionable (Mouffe, "Feminism and Radical Politics," 380). If we understand naturalized categories of identity as (nonetheless) politically contingent, then to engage a historically given identity is precisely to discern such a structure in all its partiality and provisionality, to identify its internal tendencies toward radical transformation.

8. Spillers, "Mama's Baby, Papa's Maybe," 67.

9. These "critical registers" include deconstruction (see, for example, Derrida, *Spurs: Nietzsche's Styles*); psychoanalysis (see Freud, *Beyond the Pleasure Principle*; Lacan, *Le Seminaire XX: Encore*); and feminist psychoanalysis (see Julia Kristeva, "Stabat Mater"). For a discussion of Marxist critique and liminal motherhood, see also chapters 3 and 4.

10. "Some man" would seem to refer to one or another of Melanctha's African-American lovers. But I suggest that insofar as she implicitly ascribes to him a will to know Melanctha's story "wholly," Stein assimilates Melanctha's interlocutor to a "generic" masculine, or white patriarchal position.

11. My formulation is designed to suggest a continuity or correlation between Lacan's placement of "woman" *vis-à-vis* the symbolic, and Stein's placement of black women. The stakes for both lie in producing a position of symbolic mastery through the forced abstraction and reduction of the Other.

12. By disavowing what Melanctha has (the capacity to account for herself), rather than what she lacks, the narrator precisely inverts the logic of fetishism. In this sense, Stein's text exemplifies Lee Edelman's concept of *antifetishistic* disavowal. Edelman proposes the model with reference to "the sodomitical scene," a rescripting of the primal scene, he argues, in which the penetrated body remains unmarked by castration/loss. Thus, with respect to "the sodomitical scene," the logic of fetishism is inverted: the spectator's accommodation to paternal law entails a disavowal of *excess,* of what the penetrated body all too plainly possesses. See Edelman, "Seeing Things," 107.

13. See for example Hartz, *The Liberal Tradition in America*; Pocock, *The Machiavellian Moment*; Jehlen, "New World Epics."

14. Jehlen, *American Incarnation,* 4–5.

15. Ibid., 3. Emphasis added.

16. See Carolyn Porter's deft and in many ways definitive critique of American ahistoricism in *Seeing and Being.* Porter shows compellingly how the myth of America as lacking history functions to occlude the specificity of American social conditions. Rather than acknowledge that the circumstances of capitalist development were different in the U.S., that unimpeded capitalist expansion produced a different set of social conditions, the compulsively repeated comparison to Europe serves merely to rediscover lack. As Porter puts it, "[w]hat we need to understand is that if America is different, it is not only because of what it has lacked, but also because of *what that lack has fostered*—a social reality . . . breeding an extreme form of alienation" (Porter, 20, emphasis added). I would add here, however, that it seems to me equally important to interrogate the notion of *original* lack: it does not follow from the absence of historically determined competing *class* interests that we can identify no sites of resistance or potential resistance. The point is rather that the dominant class asserted its interests, against those of the Native American or the African-American, for example, with exceptional violence.

Porter cites Louis Hartz's claim that, by the beginning of the nineteenth century, "the only insurgency required of the American middle class was that which was necessary to 'remove' the Indians, a task which, as Hartz explains, differs from 'the destruction of an order to which one belongs oneself,' because the first 'can actually be completed,' while the second 'goes on in a sense forever.'" While I appreciate Hartz's desire to distinguish between class struggle and genocide, I resist the closure he seeks to impose on the Native American's "removal." Surely the systematic extermination of America's indigenous peoples has never ceased to demand a reckoning.

17. Jefferson, *Notes on the State of Virginia,* 129. Hereafter cited as *Notes.*

18. For a discussion of the incorporation of heterogeneity as style in postmodern culture, see bell hooks, *Black Looks,* chapter 2.

19. It is helpful to consider here Ernesto Laclau's and Chantal Mouffe's conception of radical democratic politics in *Hegemony and Socialist Strategy,* in which the political is conceived as the locus of continuing contestation, while achieved consensus designates its horizon.

20. Lukács, *History and Class Consciousness,* 117–18.

21. Adorno, *Negative Dialectics,* 21.

22. See Jacques Derrida, "Declarations of Independence." For a more detailed consideration of Derrida's argument, see chapter 2.

23. Thus it remains debatable what forms a specifically female citizenship (for instance) might assume. See Ruth H. Bloch, "The Gendered Meanings of Virtue in Revolutionary America"; Dietz, "Citizenship with a Feminist Face"; MacKinnon, *Towards a Feminist Theory of the State*; Pateman, *The Sexual Contract*; and Young, "Polity and Group Difference." Less directly or exclusively concerned with the problem of citizenship *per se,* but productively addressing relevant issues of women's political rights, social needs and universalist norms are: Benhabib, "The Generalized and the Concrete Other"; Butler and Scott, *Feminists Theorize the Political*; and Fraser, *Unruly Practices,* especially chapters 7 and 8.

24. The attribution of authorship is Clinton Rossiter's in his introduction to *The Federalist Papers* (xi). The first line of Rossiter's essay exemplifies the aspiration to closure that marks Madison's text: "*The Federalist* is the most important work in political science that has ever been written, *or is likely ever to be written,* in the United States" (emphasis added).

25. *The Federalist,* 44 (emphasis added).

26. In the justifications for the breakaway of the American colonies, Britain is often figured as devouring mother—most famously, perhaps, in Tom Paine's *Common Sense.* But Britain as *consuming* mother *against which* an American political order asserts itself should not be identified with its inverse: the figure of the mother as produced *from within* liberal order—that is, the maternal body *consumed by* rational system.

Mother Britain enters the political discourse as an irreducibly irrational body. In this respect, *Common Sense* occupies a conceptually anterior moment, prior to the symbolic closure of the political that interests me here.

27. *The Federalist,* 58.

28. The objection has been made to me that I seem to derive psychoanalysis from an American context. It should be understood that bourgeois liberalism in the United States, while differently realized, emerges from the same Enlightenment tradition as, and remains fundamentally related to, its European avatars. I see no contradiction in both acknowledging the specificity of American social and political forms, and drawing on European critiques of rational order and bourgeois subjectivity.

29. In this sense, I take issue with Iris Marion Young's interpretation of the domestic woman's affect: "The bourgeois world instituted a moral division of labor between reason and sentiment, identifying masculinity with reason and femininity with sentiment, desire, and the needs of the body. [. . .] In his social scheme, for example, Rousseau excluded women from the public realm of citizenship because they are the caretakers of affectivity, desire and the body. If we allowed appeals to desires and bodily needs to move public debates, we would undermine public deliberation by fragmenting its unity" (Young, 253–54). In this otherwise nuanced and insightful essay, Young suggests that women's heterogeneity with respect to rational political order rendered feminine "affectivity" disruptive. On the contrary, I emphasize the extent to which feminine/maternal affectivity *served the project of social unity and political closure,* precisely because her affect was not heard to speak to the woman's *own* desires and "bodily needs."

30. Lacoue-Labarthe and Nancy, "Le Retrait du Politique," 193. My translation.

31. Fraser, 79.

32. Lacoue-Labarthe and Nancy, "Retrait," 187.

33. Ibid., 193.

34. Ibid., 195.

35. Lacoue-Labarthe and Nancy, "Rejouer le Politique," 26. My translation.

36. For a related discussion of this "gift," see Joan Copjec, who aligns the "cause" of the subject with the maternal body by reference to Lacan: "This indeterminate something (referred to by Lacan as object a) that causes the subject has historical specificity (it is the product of a specific discursive order) but no historical content" ("Cutting Up," 238–39).

37. Lacoue-Labarthe and Nancy, "Rejouer," 195.

38. For a related discussion of what it may mean to engage with the unrepresented, see chapter 5.

39. Fraser, 88.

40. Mitchell Breitwieser has argued persuasively that Jefferson neither homogenizes nor disjoins experience and theory, but produces an "antithetical unity," in which rational order bears the contradiction of the material.

Breitwieser takes issue with Robert Ferguson's and Wayne Franklin's "either/or" construction "of a Jefferson forced to choose between the chaos of the real and the insular solacing/stifling enclave of form and clarity," as though "to discover contradiction is also to discover a disunified and incoherent Jefferson." Rather, Breitwieser advances the alternative of "a mind simultaneously allied with the consolidating tendencies of hypothesis *and* the interruptive power of the real" (Breitwieser, "Jefferson's Prospects," 324). While embracing this reading, I nevertheless want to insist that Jefferson's entry on the black albino women marks a moment of real crisis: these women appear less to interrupt Jefferson's hypothesizing than to bring to a sudden and potentially irreversible halt the machinery of rational speculation altogether.

Breitwieser's reading of Jefferson implicitly engages the differences between Jefferson's position and Madison's in ways I in effect elide—chiefly because my argument is not so much about Jefferson as about the meaning of his albino women *vis-à-vis* the project of liberal founding broadly conceived. Thus, for instance, Breitwieser attributes to Jefferson the historical self-consciousness of which Madison in *The Federalist* seeks to disburden himself. As he puts it, Jefferson's "maintenance of an antithetical unity between theorization and attention to the complex real object demonstrates a mind conscious of itself as a historically specific set of attitudes and purposes, rather than a pure gaze" (339). However, the Jefferson I encounter in his representation of the black albino women is not simply compelled to take account of his own positionality in a world of "complex real objects," but one of not-quite-objects, which threaten to evade or to deauthorize Jefferson's surveillance.

41. It is, of course, traditional to distinguish between Federalism and Jeffersonian Republicanism. However, the advocates of political centralization and decentralization alike apprehend the task of instituting political order as the task of conceiving a *rational system* of government. With respect to the closure of the political as it concerns me here, the distinction is not immediately pertinent.

42. Of course, Jefferson falsely implies the patriarchal organization of all Native American cultures.

43. Breitwieser observes this impulse with respect to the architecture of Monticello. "The ingenuities at Monticello," he observes, "presume a slave economy while simultaneously expurgating signs of labor as often as possible: the hidden stairways; the slave passages to the kitchen; laundry and stables hidden (not 'sheltered' as Dos Passos contends) beneath the terraces; the dumbwaiters, invisible within the fireplace, that obviate the need to have wine carried into the room; the ladder that folds so that it does not look like

a ladder; and the seeming door that revolves to reveal shelves of hot food, but conceals the servers" (Breitwieser, 317).

44. Since the black woman has no legitimate authority to refuse him sexual access, the white man's sexual relation to her is by definition coercive, and the black woman's resistance always self-author(iz)ed and subversive.

45. This juridical determination of race dates to the late seventeenth and early eighteenth centuries—to 1662 in Virginia, for example; to 1705 in New York. (Higginbotham, "In the Matter of Color," 43, 127.)

2. Charlotte Temple's Remains

1. Fiedler, *Love and Death in the American Novel,* 95.

2. Cited by Davidson, in the editor's introduction to *Charlotte Temple,* xiv.

3. Williams, "Film Bodies," 10–11.

4. Derrida, "Declarations of Independence," 10.

5. For a helpful unpacking of the ideological "mirror couple" particular/general interest in Rousseau's *Social Contract,* see Althusser, *Montesquieu, Rousseau, Marx,* 146–54.

6. Most recently, Lauren Berlant has expanded on this familiar feminist critique in terms particularly relevant to my discussion. See "National Brands/National Bodies," 112–13.

7. Cited in Davidson, *Revolution and the Word,* 51.

8. Cited in Kerber, *Women of the Republic,* 246.

9. Fiedler, 95.

10. Butler, *Gender Trouble,* 50.

11. Such a loss of political identity, of course, represents a loss, *not* of anything this readership actually possessed prior to the installation of a national order, but rather the loss of a *possibility* that seemed (as Kerber documents) to attend the formation of a democratic regime.

12. Kaja Silverman offers an excellent account of how psychoanalysis and cinema displace the masculine subject's interiority onto the woman/mother, in order to ensure his discursive authority. See *The Acoustic Mirror,* chapter 3. See also my chapter 3.

13. Susanna Rowson, *Charlotte Temple,* 14. Hereafter cited as *CT.*

14. See Kerber, especially chapter 9. For Kerber, "Republican Motherhood" represents a more enlightened construction of feminine identity than "the Enlightenment" itself produced: in defining the mother as the cultivator of patriotic offspring, she argues, "the ideology of Republican Motherhood seemed to accomplish what the Enlightenment had not by identifying the intersection of the woman's private domain and the polis" (283). Thus "it justified women's absorption and participation in the civic culture" (284), furnished a

strategy for politicizing women's role even as republican law barred their participation in the political order. My use of the term diverges from the author's; I contend that the ideology of Republican Motherhood reflects rather than compromises or moderates the logic of women's exclusion from the emergent political order. For a fuller discussion of Kerber's argument, see chapter 1.

15. My use of "abjection" follows Julia Kristeva's elaboration of the term in *Powers of Horror.* Kristeva's notion of abjection is at least partially consonant with what Irigaray invokes under the concept of "dereliction," as elaborated in *Ethique de la différence sexuelle.* For Irigaray, women are in a state of dereliction because they lack a symbolic, remain unsymbolized within the phallogocentric order. With and against these theorists, my project here is to historicize the conditions of women's abject or derelict relation to the social symbolic, which threatens to assume in both Kristeva and Irigaray a kind of transhistorical and/or global reference. By under- or de-historicizing women's relation to the symbolic, by failing to specify which "women" we mean, we risk essentializing the very formations we seek to unravel.

16. Cathy Davidson has argued that Rowson shifts the burden of moral responsibility from Charlotte to her society: "She is a victim not so much of her wayward desires but of a shoddy education, of evil advisers (including one schoolteacher), of her legal and social inferiority" (*Revolution and the Word,* 137). But in Rowson's indictment of Charlotte's society, I read more particularly a critique of privatized femininity, which renders Charlotte, from the moment she leaves the women's sphere, incapable of willed action either with or against the prescriptions of "duty."

17. See Davidson, *Revolution and the Word,* 140ff.

18. Cathy Davidson shows persuasively that in transforming the sermonizing newspaper accounts of Whitman's death into Eliza Wharton's story, Hannah Foster restores "the complexity of which she [Whitman] had been deprived in the early allegories of her life and death" (*Revolution and the Word,* 143). While Davidson reads Foster as militating against the reduction of Elizabeth Whitman's narrative to Charlotte Temple's, I want to explore the (complementary) ways in which *Charlotte Temple,* and the graveyard spectacle which it produces, are the necessary pre-texts to this novel about the possibilities and limitations of women's community.

19. Hannah Foster, *The Coquette,* 31. Hereafter cited as *CQ.*

3. Revivification and Utopian Time

1. Ernst Bloch, *The Utopian Function of Art and Literature,* 121.

2. Ernst Bloch, 120.

3. For a complementary discussion of Walter Benjamin and the gendering of history, see chapter 4.

4. Thus I read the notable obscurity of Bloch's phrasing in this passage as the mark of his disavowal. Bloch blinds himself to the historical specificity of his critical practice at the very moment he is poised to acknowledge it.

5. It is helpful to compare Bloch's formulation of the utopian, as the "non-mythological surplus" of particular cultural signifiers, with Julia Kristeva's notion of the maternal, as a "heterogeneity that cannot be subsumed in the signifier" (Kristeva, "Stabat Mater," 259). For Bloch, unlike Kristeva, the utopian/maternal *inhabits* specific cultural codes, as a possibility historically *intrinsic* to them.

6. Fuller, *Women in the Nineteenth Century,* 49–51.

7. Stansell, *City of Women,* 66.

8. While I agree, then, with Hazel Carby's assertion that "the conventions of True Womanhood" serve to uphold a "racist, ideological system" (Carby, *Reconstructing Womanhood,* 50), I suggest that the discourse of sentimentalism is not finally *reducible* to the discourse of True Womanhood, though it does, certainly, *participate* in its fundamentally racist and classist assumptions. However, the extent to which nineteenth century African-American writers could appropriate and radically *reconfigure* sentimental narrative models argues for sentimentalism's dialogical structures.

9. Douglas, *The Feminization of American Culture,* passim.

10. Poe, "Ligeia," 190–92. Hereafter cited as *LG.*

11. Silverman, *The Acoustic Mirror,* 105.

12. Irwin, *American Hieroglyphics,* 227.

13. Pease, *Visionary Compacts,* 189.

14. Ibid., 190.

15. With the notable exception of Daniel Hoffman, none of Poe's critics have remarked Ligeia's maternal characteristics. While Hoffman acknowledges Ligeia's function as "Mother-Figure" in the tale, he situates the narrator's relation to her within a strictly oedipal frame. The narrator's "problem," in Hoffman's analysis, turns out to be Poe's impotence.

16. Stowe, *Uncle Tom's Cabin,* 528. Hereafter cited as *UTC.*

17. Interpreted in this way, Legree's violence should remind us of Margaret Homans's revisionist claim: "The symbolic order is founded, not merely on the regrettable loss of the mother, but on her active and overt murder" (Homans, *Bearing the Word,* 11).

4. "Strange Coincidence"

1. Julia Kristeva's *claiming* of "monumental time" as a "trans-European" or global time for women in her influential essay "Women's Time," represents, of course, a different answer to the problem of women in/and history ("Women's Time," 189, 190). As my argument here should suggest, this

spatialized or eternalized time strikes me as profoundly contaminated by the logic of Western linear history, and as such, a suspect model of a multicultural temporality.

2. Freud, "Some Psychical Consequences of the Anatomical Distinction between the Sexes," 191.

3. Freud, "The Splitting of the Ego," 373–74.

4. Freud, "Fetishism," 200.

5. Brunswick, as cited in Laplanche and Pontalis, 311.

6. Elizabeth Grosz, "Lesbian Fetishism?" 43–44. Hereafter cited as *LF.*

7. Lacan, "The Object Relation and the Intersubjective Relation," 217.

8. Lacan makes the point most famously in "The Signification of the Phallus":

> The phenomenology that emerges from analytic experience is certainly of a kind to demonstrate in desire the paradoxical, deviant, erratic, eccentric, even scandalous character by which it is distinguished from need [. . .] This is why we must articulate [the status of desire] here, beginning with *demand,* whose proper characteristics are eluded in the notion of frustration (which Freud never used).
>
> Demand in itself bears on something other than the satisfactions it calls for. It is demand of a presence or of an absence—which is what is manifested in the primordial relation to the mother, *pregnant with that Other to be situated within the needs that it can satisfy.* Demand constitutes the Other as already possessing the "privilege" of satisfying needs, that is to say, the power of depriving them of that alone by which they are satisfied. This privilege of the Other thus outlines the radical form of the gift of that which the Other does not have, namely, its love. (*Ecrits,* 286, emphasis added)

Thus Lacan invokes "the primordial relation" to the mother only as/at the horizon where intersubjectivity appears: the primordial mother is "pregnant" with that M/Other whose discontinuity or difference from the child appears, not insofar as she must inevitably fail in the perfect satisfaction of the child's needs, but precisely because she is capable of satisfying need, possesses the "privilege" of granting or withholding satisfaction. As a result, whatever she offers in the way of satisfaction is "transmut[ed] into a proof of love," and indeed to the very extent that she satisfies need, her gestures "are reduced (*sich erniedrigt*) to the level of being no more than the *crushing* of the demand for love. . . ." The *demand* for satisfaction is in and of itself excessive with respect to anything that effects completion (and so with respect to much of what is celebrated in the iconography of maternal "nurture").

9. Lacan, "The Object Relation and the Intersubjective Relation," 218.

10. Jacqueline Rose offers one of the subtlest and very nearly compelling versions of this claim, although she radically understates the extent to which Lacan shores up the logic of patriarchy even as he separates possession of the phallus from anatomical determinations. See *Sexuality in the Field of Vision*, especially chapter 2.

11. Jessica Benjamin's interesting model of the mother/child relation in "A Desire of One's Own: Psychoanalytic Feminism and Intersubjective Space" suggests how we might theorize the child's position at this juncture. Neither continuous with the mother, nor autonomous on the model of the rational bourgeois subject, the child inhabits a space in the mother's proximity, neither under her gaze nor outside her purview, where s/he remains "alone in the presence of the other" (94). In this field of "play," which arguably represents Benjamin's rescripting of the fort/da game, the child occupies him or herself in various interrogations of his or her relation to the world, but periodically turns to the mother for assurance of her sponsoring presence.

12. In this sense, Grosz's argument evokes Derrida's model of generalized fetishism. For Derrida, the fetish in its "undecidable mobility" exceeds the structure of the opposition "true/nontrue, substitute/nonsubstitute, denial/affirmation and so on" (*Glas*, 211). At stake in Grosz's model of lesbian fetishism, however, is not only the possibility of destabilizing the "truth" of women's lack, but of articulating an alternative narrative of feminine subjectivity. For Grosz, what is ultimately interesting is the *alterity* of the fetish with respect to social-symbolic reality, rather than its *undecidability*.

13. In an unpublished lecture on *Citizen Kane,* "From Log Cabin to Xanadu," Laura Mulvey suggestively links this form of fetishism to fascism, and its preservation for political purposes of a phantasmatic and congealed past.

14. Freud, "Fetishism," 198, 200.

15. Hawthorne, *The Blithedale Romance,* 17. Hereafter cited as *BR*.

16. Brodhead, *Melville, Hawthorne and the Novel,* 115.

17. Roof, *A Lure of Knowledge,* 93.

18. Cummins, *The Lamplighter,* 12. Hereafter cited as *L.*

19. Cited in Silverman, 74.

5. "Your Mother Is Here"

1. Spillers, "Interstices," passim.

2. Carby, *Reconstructing Womanhood,* 49.

3. Smith, "The Loophole of Retreat," 213.

4. Ibid., 219.

5. Spivak, "Can the Subaltern Speak?" 279.

6. Spillers, "Interstices," 76–77.

7. Ibid., 89.

8. A debarment that we might theorize as abjection (following Kristeva) or dereliction (following Irigaray), insofar as the discourses of race and gender converge, and we might want to claim that the status of the African-American is structurally similar or analogous to the status of the white woman. Of course, the burden of this chapter, indeed of this book, is precisely to suggest that this analogy does not hold, that the domesticated white woman remains interior to rationalized structures of power in ways that the commodified African-American does not. At a minimum, then, I would suggest that if gender can only be thought at its points of intersection with race, class, ethnicity, and sexuality, then we need to learn to theorize abjections and derelictions.

9. Spivak, 294.

10. See Spillers, "Mama's Baby, Papa's Maybe: An American Grammar Book."

11. Spivak, 282.

12. Ranajit Guha, as cited in Spivak, 284.

13. Spivak, 285.

14. Jacobs, *Incidents in the Life of a Slave Girl,* 1. Hereafter cited as I.

15. My argument thus converges with Houston A. Baker's argument on African-American slave narratives, in which, he contends, emancipation is represented as a process of self-commodification. The narrators of these texts produce themselves as subjects in a specific way, "convert[ing] property, through property, into humanity" (Baker, *Blues, Ideology,* 48).

16. The work of bell hooks, most recently her essay on "The Politics of Radical Black Subjectivity," has helped to focus my attention on the process of "becoming subject." Drawing on hooks in a recent public address, Patricia Hill Collins identified this place of becoming as a site for black feminist theorizing. Collins thus locates in the movement from commodity to subject, or (as I am calling it) decommodification, the conditions for the production of alternative black feminist knowledges.

17. Spivak, 295.

18. Ibid., 287

19. In what has become the conventional usage, I distinguish between Harriet Jacobs, the author of *Incidents,* and Linda Brent, the protagonist of Jacobs's narrative.

20. At the other moment in the narrative where "the delicate silence of womanly sympathy" is invoked to signify an affective bond between African-American women, it suggestively follows Linda Brent's first encounter with the visual representation of a person of color. Newly arrived in Philadelphia, Brent is taken by a friend to an artist's studio, to be shown the portraits of her

children which the friend had commissioned. "I had never seen any paintings of colored people before," Brent remarks, "and they seemed to me beautiful" (*I* 162). Thus Brent's recourse to the sentimental discourse of "delicate silence" is introduced by the remark that the African-American subject is as such, and in her specificity, only rarely the subject of representation.

21. Baker, 53.

22. Smith, 212.

23. For a discussion of the visual as the privileged register of intersubjective relations in psychoanalytic theory, see chapter 4.

24. In this sense, Tawanna Brown proposes, "instead of Linda's mother acting as the authorial voice, the children serve the maternal function" ("Rehearing Voices," unpublished paper). Brown argues for the interdependence of mother and children in *Incidents,* so that motherhood in this model is not prior to intersubjectivity, but rather constituted in it.

Postscript

1. Doane, "Technophilia," 166.

2. Langton, "Artificial Life," 38–39.

3. Hollinger, "Cybernetic Deconstructions," 207.

4. Gordon, "Ying and Yang Duke It Out," 199.

5. Doane, 174.

6. Murphy, "Is Pregnancy Necessary?" 81–82.

7. Cited in Hartouni, "Containing Women," 46.

8. Ibid., 49.

9. Murphy often approaches the question of ectogenesis in what would seem to be a purely hypothetical register, which disturbingly both circles and brackets issues of social class. Thus, for instance, she reflects that "a woman may find ectogenesis desirable because she is a smoker, drug-user or casual drinker" or because "her job may be hazardous for pregnant women." Implicitly, at such moments, Murphy posits broad access to this technology for women from all social classes; yet the term "casual" nevertheless recontains the complicating factors she enumerates within a comfortably middle-class frame, while the only careers she enumerates are "athletics, dancing, modelling, acting."

10. Hartouni, 46.

11. While Doane never directly alludes to Laura Mulvey here, her construction of technological fetishism both recalls the totalizing logic of Mulvey's famous argument in "Visual Pleasure and Narrative Cinema," and often seems to align technological fetishism with the pleasure of the gaze—to align technophilia with scopophilia.

12. Psychoanalysis is, of course, a discourse of Western bourgeois subjectivity, of a specific historical configuration which this discipline elevates to the status of a universal. My investment here is in the possibility of dislodging feminist psychoanalysis from its Western supremacist frame, which means, among other things, in the possibility of deploying psychoanalytic models to denaturalize and decenter the bourgeois subject.

13. See Hortense Spillers, "Mama's Baby, Papa's Maybe: An American Grammar Book." Other important critical models of alternative configurations of motherhood include Christine Stansell, *City of Women: Sex and Class in New York, 1789–1860,* especially chapters 6 and 10; Cherrie Moraga, "From a Long Line of Vendidas: Chicanas and Feminism."

14. See Madelon Sprengnether's insightful reading of *Beyond,* and Freud's retrogressive advance toward the figure of the mother he seeks to elide, in *The Spectral Mother.*

15. Penley and Ross, "Cyborgs at Large: Interview with Donna Haraway," 20.

16. Gibson, *Neuromancer,* 51. Hereafter cited as *N.*

17. Ross, *Strange Weather,* 153.

18. Implicitly, then, in a cyberpunk world, gender is organized, not in terms of possession/lack, but of access/debarment, a binary that can less readily be made to derive from the literal distinctions of sex. While the "cyberspace cowboys" of Gibson's, and indeed most cyberpunk novels, are exclusively male, the female hackers of Pat Cadigan's novel *Synners,* for example, suggest how the sex/gender system can be productively destabilized within this model.

19. A doubling and negation which Lacan has theorized as the mirror stage. Most pertinent for my argument here is the infant's proto-disavowal of the body's disarticulations and contingency that the contemplation of the specular image is seen to enable.

20. It is arguably toward such a destabilization of knowledge that what Naomi Schor defines as female fetishism would tend. Following Sarah Kofman, Schor suggests that "what is pertinent to women in fetishism is the paradigm of undecidability that it offers. By appropriating the fetishist's oscillation between denial and recognition of castration, women can effectively counter any move to reduce their bisexuality to a single one of its poles." Linda Lee's techno-fetishization, traceable, through Neuromancer, to a deceased Marie-France, instantiates Schor's model in a particularly suggestive way. Marie-France's fetishizing of the female body transfers the locus of the undecidability she plainly privileges, from the masculine fetishist, who disavows the ostensibly verifiable truth of women's lack, to a (female-programmed) AI, who engenders a female body beyond phallocentric categories of knowledge. See Schor, "Female Fetishism," 363–72.

21. Haraway, "A Manifesto for Cyborgs," 203.

22. Penley and Ross, 20.

23. Temporary—but also *timely*, if we consider, for instance, that the same post-humanist science fiction narratives which have popularized the figure of the cyborg, or, more generally, labored to imagine partial, hybridized, decentered identities (*The Terminator*, perhaps most spectacularly, but most recently *Aliens 3*), tend simultaneously to reinscribe essentialized motherhood (and the structures of identity it underwrites). Under these circumstances, it seems to me as important for feminist criticism to search out where and how motherhood might be dislodged from its essentialized frame, as to privilege the figure of the non-maternal woman.

24. See Thomas Foster, "Meat Puppets or Robopaths? Cyberpunk and the Question of Embodiment."

25. My appreciation of this passage in the narrative owes much to N. Katherine Hayles's observation, at a session of the Society for Literature and Science Annual Conference (Montreal, 1992), that cyberspace is hardly the achievement of disembodied subjectivity, when the virtual reality enthusiast is precisely a body *loaded down* with equipment—a body all the more conspicuous for its (supposed) irrelevance.

Works Cited

Adorno, Theodor W. *Negative Dialectics*. Trans. E. B. Ashton. New York: Continuum, 1973.

Althusser, Louis. *Montesquieu, Rousseau, Marx: Politics and History*. Trans. Ben Brewster. London: Verso, 1982.

Anzaldúa, Gloria. *Borderlands/La Frontera: The New Mestiza*. San Francisco: aunt lute, 1987.

Baker, Houston A., Jr. *Blues, Ideology and Afro-American Literature: A Vernacular Theory*. Chicago: University of Chicago Press, 1984.

Benhabib, Seyla. "The Generalized and the Concrete Other: The Kohlberg-Gilligan Controversy and Feminist Theory." In *Feminism as Critique*. Ed. Seyla Benhabib and Drucilla Cornell. Minneapolis: University of Minnesota Press, 1988.

Benjamin, Jessica. "A Desire of One's Own: Psychoanalytic Feminism and Intersubjective Space." In *Feminist Studies/Critical Studies*. Ed. Teresa de Lauretis. Bloomington: Indiana University Press, 1986.

Benjamin, Walter. *Illuminations*. Ed. Hannah Arendt. Trans. Harry Zohn. New York: Schocken, 1969.

Berlant, Lauren. "National Brands/National Bodies." In *Comparative American Identities: Race, Sex and Nationality in the Modern Text*. Ed. Hortense J. Spillers. New York: Routledge, Chapman and Hall, 1991.

Bloch, Ernst. *The Utopian Function of Art and Literature*. Trans. Jack Zipes and Frank Mecklenburg. Cambridge, Mass.: MIT Press, 1988.

Bloch, Ruth. "The Gendered Meanings of Virtue in Revolutionary America." *Signs* 13 (1987).

Breitwieser, Mitchell. "Jefferson's Prospects." *Prospects: An Annual Journal of American Cultural Studies* 10 (1985).

Brodhead, Richard. *Melville, Hawthorne and the Novel*. Chicago: University of Chicago Press, 1973.

Brown, Tawanna. "Rehearing Voices and Visions of Motherhood in Harriet Jacobs' *Incidents in the Life of a Slave Girl.*" Unpublished paper.

Butler, Judith. *Gender Trouble: Feminism and the Subversion of Identity.* New York: Routledge, 1990.

Butler, Judith, and Joan W. Scott, eds. *Feminists Theorize the Political.* New York: Routledge, 1992.

Cadigan, Pat. *Synners.* New York: Bantam, 1991.

Carby, Hazel V. *Reconstructing Womanhood: The Emergence of the Afro-American Novelist.* Oxford: Oxford University Press, 1987.

Collins, Patricia Hill. "Knowledge and Power: The Challenge of Black Feminist Thought." Lecture delivered at Indiana University, Bloomington. April 23, 1993.

Copjec, Joan. "Cutting Up." In *Between Feminism and Psychoanalysis.* Ed. Teresa Brennan. London: Routledge, 1989.

Cummins, Maria Susanna. *The Lamplighter.* Ed. Nina Baym. New Brunswick: Rutgers University Press, 1988.

Davidson, Cathy N. *Revolution and the Word: The Rise of the Novel in America.* Oxford: Oxford University Press, 1986.

Derrida, Jacques. "Declarations of Independence." Trans. Tom Keenan and Tom Pepper. *New Political Science* 15 (1986).

———. *Glas.* Trans. John P. Leavy, Jr., and Richard Rand. Lincoln: University of Nebraska Press, 1990.

———. *Spurs: Nietzsche's Styles.* Trans. Barbara Harlow. Chicago: University of Chicago Press, 1979.

Dietz, Mary. "Citizenship with a Feminist Face: The Problem with Maternal Thinking." *Political Theory* 13:1 (1985).

Dinshaw, Carolyn. "The Touch of the Queer." Paper delivered at Indiana University, Bloomington. February 10, 1994.

Doane, Mary Ann. "Technophilia: Technology, Representation and the Feminine." In *Body/Politics: Women and the Discourses of Science.* Ed. Mary Jacobus, Evelyn Fox-Keller, and Sally Shuttleworth. New York: Routledge, 1990.

Douglas, Ann. *The Feminization of American Culture.* New York: Avon, 1978.

Edelman, Lee. "Seeing Things: Representation, the Scene of Surveillance and the Spectacle of Gay Male Sex." In *Inside/Out.* Ed. Diana Fuss. New York: Routledge, 1991.

Fiedler, Leslie A. *Love and Death in the American Novel.* New York: Stein and Day, 1966.

Foster, Hannah. *The Coquette.* Ed. Cathy N. Davidson. Oxford: Oxford University Press, 1986.

Foster, Thomas. "Meat Puppets of Robopaths? Cyberpunk and the Question of Embodiment." *Genders* (1993).

Fraser, Nancy. *Unruly Practices: Power, Discourse and Gender in Contemporary Social Theory.* Minneapolis: University of Minnesota Press, 1989.

Freud, Sigmund. *Beyond the Pleasure Principle.* In The Standard Edition of the Complete Works of Sigmund Freud. Vol. 18. Ed. James Strachey. Trans. James Strachey. London: Hogarth, 1974.

———. "Fetishism." In *Collected Papers.* Vol. 5. Ed. James Strachey. Trans. Joan Riviere. New York: Basic, 1959.

———. "Some Psychical Consequences of the Anatomical Distinction between the Sexes." In *Collected Papers.* Vol. 5. Trans. James Strachey.

———. "The Splitting of the Ego in the Defensive Process." In *Collected Papers.* Vol. 5. Trans. James Strachey.

Fuller, Margaret. *Woman in the Nineteenth Century.* New York: Norton, 1971.

Gibson, William. *Neuromancer.* New York: Ace, 1984.

Gordon, Joan. "Ying and Yang Duke It Out." In *Storming the Reality Studio.* Ed. Larry McCaffrey. Durham: Duke University Press, 1991.

Grosz, Elizabeth. "Lesbian Fetishism?" *Differences: A Journal of Feminist Cultural Studies* 3:2 (1991).

Haraway, Donna J. "A Manifesto for Cyborgs." In *Feminism/Postmodernism.* Ed. Linda J. Nicholson. New York: Routledge, 1990.

Hartouni, Valerie. "Containing Women: Reproductive Discourse in the 1980's." In *Technoculture.* Ed. Constance Penley and Andrew Ross. Minneapolis: University of Minnesota Press, 1991.

Hartz, Louis. *The Liberal Tradition in America.* New York: Harcourt, Brace and World, 1955.

Hawthorne, Nathaniel. *The Blithedale Romance.* New York: Penguin, 1985.

Higginbotham, Leon A., Jr. *In the Matter of Color: Race and the American Legal Process.* New York: Oxford University Press, 1978.

Hoffman, Daniel. *Poe Poe Poe Poe Poe Poe Poe.* Garden City, N.Y.: Doubleday, 1972.

Hollinger, Veronica. "Cybernetic Deconstructions: Cyberpunk and Postmodernism." In *Storming the Reality Studio.* Ed. Larry McCaffrey. Durham: Duke University Press, 1991.

Homans, Margaret. *Bearing the Word: Language and Female Experience in Nineteenth Century Women's Writing.* Chicago: University of Chicago Press, 1986.

hooks, bell. *Yearning: Race, Gender and Cultural Politics.* Boston: South End Press, 1990.

———. *Black Looks: Race and Representation.* Boston: South End Press, 1992.

Irigaray, Luce. *Ethique de la Différence Sexuelle.* Paris: Minuit, 1984.

Irwin, John. *American Hieroglyphics.* Baltimore: Johns Hopkins University Press, 1983.

Jacobs, Harriet. *Incidents in the Life of a Slave Girl.* Ed. Jean Fagan Yellin. Cambridge, Mass.: Harvard University Press, 1987.

Jameson, Frederic. *Postmodernism, Or the Cultural Logic of Late Capitalism.* Durham: Duke University Press, 1991.

Jefferson, Thomas. *Notes on the State of Virginia.* Ed. William Peden. New York: Norton, 1972.

Jehlen, Myra. "New World Epics: The Middle Class Novel in America." *Salmagundi* 36 (1977).

———. *American Incarnation: The Individual, the Nation and the Continent.* Cambridge, Mass.: MIT Press, 1986.

Kerber, Linda K. *Women of the Republic: Intellect and Ideology in Revolutionary America.* New York: Norton, 1981.

Kristeva, Julia. *Powers of Horror.* Trans. Leon S. Roudiez. New York: Columbia University Press, 1982.

———. "Stabat Mater." In *Tales of Love.* Trans Leon S. Roudiez. New York: Columbia University Press, 1987.

———. "Women's Time." In *The Kristeva Reader.* Ed. Toril Moi. New York: Columbia University Press, 1986.

Lacan, Jacques. *Le Seminaire XX: Encore.* Paris: Seuil, 1975.

———. "The Object Relation and the Intersubjective Relation." In *The Seminar of Jacques Lacan.* Vol. 1. Ed. Jacques-Alain Miller. Trans. John Forrester. New York: Norton, 1988.

———. "The Signification of the Phallus." In *Ecrits.* Trans. Alan Sheridan. New York: Norton, 1977.

Laclau, Ernesto, and Chantal Mouffe. *Hegemony and Socialist Strategy: Towards a Radical Democratic Politics.* London: Verso, 1985.

Lacoue-Labarthe, Philippe, and Jean-Luc Nancy. "Rejouer le Politique." *Travaux du Centre de Recherches Philosophiques sur le Politique.* Paris: Galilee, 1981.

———. "Le Retrait du Politique." *Travaux du Centre de Recherches Philosophiques sur le Politique.* Paris: Galilee, 1983.

Langton, Christopher. "Artificial Life." In *Artificial Life.* Santa Fe Institute Studies in the Sciences of Complexity. New York: Addison-Wesley, 1988.

Laplanche, Jean, and J-B Pontalis. *The Language of Psychoanalysis.* Trans. Donald Nicholson-Smith. New York: Norton, 1973.

Lorde, Audre. *Zami: A New Spelling of My Name.* Freedom, Calif.: Crossing Press, 1982.

Lukács, Georg. *History and Class Consciousness.* Trans. Rodney Livingston. Cambridge, Mass.: MIT Press, 1988.

MacKinnon, Catharine. *Toward a Feminist Theory of the State.* Cambridge, Mass.: Harvard University Press, 1989.

Madison, James, et al. *The Federalist Papers.* Ed. Clinton Rossiter. New York: New American Library, 1961.

Moraga, Cherrie. "From a Long Line of Vendidas: Chicanas and Feminism." In *Feminist Studies/Critical Studies.* Ed. Teresa de Lauretis. Bloomington: Indiana University Press, 1986.

Mouffe, Chantal. "Feminism and Radical Politics." In *Feminists Theorize the Political.* Ed. Judith Butler and Joan W. Scott. New York: Routledge, 1992.

Mulvey, Laura. "Visual Pleasure and Narrative Cinema." In *Visual and Other Pleasures.* Bloomington: Indiana University Press, 1989.

———. "From Log Cabin to Xanadu: Psychoanalytic Approaches to *Citizen Kane.*" Unpublished paper delivered at Indiana University, Bloomington. November 16, 1992.

Murphy, Julien. "Is Pregnancy Necessary? Feminist Concerns about Ectogenesis." *Hypatia: A Journal of Feminist Philosophy* 4:3 (1989).

Paine, Tom. *Common Sense.* Ed. Thomas Wendel. New York: Barron's Educational Series, 1975.

Pateman, Carole. *The Sexual Contract.* Stanford: Stanford University Press, 1988.

Pease, Donald. *Visionary Compacts: American Renaissance Writing in Cultural Context.* Madison: University of Wisconsin Press, 1987.

Penley, Constance, and Andrew Ross. "Cyborgs at Large: Interview with Donna Haraway." In *Technoculture.* Minneapolis: University of Minnesota Press, 1991.

Pocock, J. G. A. *The Machiavellian Moment: Florentine Political Thought and the Atlantic Republican Tradition.* Princeton: Princeton University Press, 1975.

Poe, Edgar Allan. "Ligeia." In *Great Short Works of Edgar Allan Poe.* New York: Harper & Row, 1970.

Porter, Carolyn. *Seeing and Being: The Plight of the Participant Observer in Emerson, James, Adams and Faulkner.* Middletown: Wesleyan University Press, 1981.

Roof, Judith. *A Lure of Knowledge: Lesbian Sexuality and Theory.* New York: Columbia University Press, 1991.

Rose, Jacqueline. *Sexuality in the Field of Vision.* London: Verso, 1986.

Ross, Andrew. *Strange Weather: Culture, Science and Technology in the Age of Limits.* New York: Verso, 1991.

Rowson, Susanna. *Charlotte Temple.* Ed. Cathy N. Davidson. Oxford: Oxford University Press, 1986.

Schor, Naomi. "Female Fetishism." In *The Female Body in Western Culture.* Ed. Susan Rubin Suleiman. Cambridge, Mass.: Harvard University Press, 1986.

Silverman, Kaja. *The Acoustic Mirror: The Female Voice in Psychoanalysis and Cinema.* Bloomington: Indiana University Press, 1988.

Smith, Valerie. "The Loophole of Retreat." In *Reading Black, Reading Feminist: A Critical Anthology.* Ed. Henry Louis Gates, Jr. New York: Meridian, 1990.

Spillers, Hortense. "Interstices: A Small Drama of Words." In *Pleasure and Danger.* Ed. Carole S. Vance. New York: Routledge, 1984.

———. "Mama's Baby, Papa's Maybe: An American Grammar Book." Diacritics 17:2 (1987).

Spivak, Gayatri Chakravorty. "Can the Subaltern Speak?" In *Marxism and the Interpretation of Culture.* Ed. Cary Nelson and Lawrence Grossberg. Urbana: University of Illinois Press, 1988.

Sprengnether, Madelon. *The Spectral Mother: Freud, Feminism and Psychoanalysis.* Ithaca: Cornell University Press, 1989.

Stansell, Christine. *City of Women: Sex and Class in New York, 1789-1860.* Urbana: University of Illinois Press, 1987.

Stowe, Harriet Beecher. *Uncle Tom's Cabin.* New York: Penguin, 1981.

Warner, Michael. "Textuality and Legitimacy in the Printed Constitution." *Proceedings of the American Antiquarian Society* 97:1 (1987).

Warner, Susan. *The Wide, Wide, World.* New York: Feminist Press, 1987.

Williams, Linda. "Film Bodies: Gender, Genre and Excess." *Film Quarterly* 44:4 (1991).

Young, Iris Marion. "Polity and Group Difference: A Critique of the Ideal of Universal Citizenship." *Ethics* 99:2 (1989).

Index

Adorno, Theodor, 8, 10
Alien 3, 147n23
Althusser, Louis, 139n5
Anzaldúa, Gloria, ix

Baker, Houston, 107, 144n15
Benhabib, Seyla, 136n23
Benjamin, Jessica, 143n11
Benjamin, Walter, x, 62–64
Berlant, Lauren, 139n6
Blade Runner, ix
Bloch, Ernst, 41–44, 46, 60, 141nn4,5
Bloch, Ruth, 136n23
Brodhead, Richard, 77
Breitwieser, Mitchell, 137–38n40,
    138–39n43
Brown, Tawanna, 145n24
Brunswick, Ruth Mack, 66–67, 87
Butler, Judith, ix, 3, 28–29, 136n23

Cadigan, Pat, 146n18
Carby, Hazel V., 93–94, 141n8
Chion, Michel, 85
Collins, Patricia Hill, 144n16
Copjec, Joan, 137n36
Coverture, 30, 32–33, 36, 39–40
Cummins, Maria Susanna, xii, 65, 83–91
Cyberpunk, 113–14, 146n18

Davidson, Cathy, 140nn16–18
Democracy and democratic sociality, ix,

xi, xiii, 2, 4, 6, 7, 12, 17, 30, 34, 44,
    134n3
Derrida, Jacques: "Declarations of
    Independence," 9, 25–26, 39, 40;
    Spurs, 134n9; *Glas,* 143n12
Dietz, Mary, 136n23
Dinshaw, Carolyn, 133n2
Doane, Mary Ann, 113, 114–15, 117,
    145nn1,5,11
Douglas, Ann, 47
Dwight, Timothy, 27–28

Ecriture feminine, viii
Edelman, Lee, 135n12
Enlightenment, x, 6, 128, 137n28
Exceptionalism, 7

Fetishism: xii, 11, 49, 62–69, 70–74,
    75, 77, 83, 88, 89–90, 91, 117–18,
    143n12, 146n20; technological
    fetishism, 113, 115, 117, 119, 122,
    123, 124–25, 126–27, 130, 131–32,
    146n20
Fiedler, Leslie, 24, 27
Fraser, Nancy, 14–16, 136n23
Foster, Hannah, xi, 38–40
Freud, Sigmund: *Beyond the Pleasure
    Principle,* 13, 118, 134n9;
    "Fetishism" and "The Splitting of
    the Ego," 62–64, 65–68, 70, 71,
    72–74, 75

Fuller, Margaret, ix, 44–46, 53, 57

Gibson, William, xii, 113–14, 117,
    119–32, 146n16
Gordon, Joan, 113–14
Gothic, 41–44
Grosz, Elizabeth, 63–65, 68, 70–74, 75,
    90, 143n12

Haraway, Donna, viii, ix, xiii, 119, 128
Hartouni, Valerie, 116–17
Hartz, Louis, 135–36n16
Hawthorne, Nathaniel, xii, 64–65,
    74–83
Hayles, Katherine, 147n25
Hoffman, Daniel, 141n15
Hollinger, Veronica, 113
Homans, Margaret, 141n17
hooks, bell, 136n18, 144n16

Irigaray, Luce, xiii, 140n15, 144n8
Irwin, John, 51–52

Jacobs, Harriet, xii, 92–94, 96–111,
    144n19
Jameson, Fredric, ix
Jefferson, Thomas, 2–3, 4, 5, 7–8,
    16–23, 137–38n40
Jehlen, Myra, 6–7, 8

Kerber, Linda, 1, 3, 12–13, 30, 134n5,
    139–40n14
Kristeva, Julia, viii, xiii, 32, 50, 134n9,
    140n15, 141n1, 144n8

Lacan, Jacques, 68–70, 134n9, 135n11,
    142nn7,8, 143nn9,10, 146n19
Laclau, Ernesto, 136n19
Lacoue-Labarthe, Philippe, 14–16
Langton, Christopher, 122
Lorde, Audre, viii
Lukács, Georg, 8

MacKinnon, Catharine, 136n23
Madison, James, 9–10, 11–12, 13, 14,

136n24, 138
Melodrama, 25–26, 104
Metz, Christian, 115
Moraga, Cherrie, 146n13
Motherhood: bourgeois (or affective),
    viii, xi, xii, xiii, 11, 12, 13–14, 31,
    42–45, 49–50, 54, 57, 78–82, 84,
    86–87, 89, 117–19; captive black, x,
    xi, 3–4, 16–17, 22–23, 56, 58–59,
    99, 102–111; non-original (or
    performative), viii, ix, 37–38, 46,
    50, 56, 59–60, 82–83, 99, 110–11,
    129–32; and technology, xii–xiii,
    113, 114–17, 118–19, 122–23, 125
Mouffe, Chantal, 133–34n3, 136n19
Mulvey, Laura, 143n13, 145n11
Murphy, Julien, 116, 145nn6,9

Nancy, Jean-Luc, 14–16

Paine, Tom, 136n26
Pateman, Carole, 136n23
Pease, Donald, 51–52
Poe, Edgar Allan, xii, 47–55, 56
Porter, Carolyn, 135–36n16
Postmodernism, viii, ix, xii
Pretenders, the, xiii

Race and racialized gender: blackness, x,
    xii, 2–4, 5, 18–20, 93–99, 144n8;
    whiteness, xi, 5, 59, 98, 99–100;
    "non/whiteness," 4, 5, 16–17,
    20–23, 56, 60. See also Motherhood
Reproductive technology. See Mother-
    hood
Republican womanhood, 1–2, 13, 29,
    30, 133–34n3, 134n5, 139–40n14
Richardson, Samuel, 27, 32
Roof, Judith, 79–80
Ross, Andrew, 120
Rossiter, Clinton, 136n24
Rowson, Susanna, xi, 24–40, 140n16
Rush, Benjamin, 27

Schor, Naomi, 146n20

Sentimentalism: x, xi, xii, 12, 13, 22,
    25, 29–30, 32, 33, 36, 37, 40,
    42–44, 46–47, 60, 84, 106, 114,
    123, 134n5; masculinist inflections
    of, 49, 50, 54; African-American
    inflections of, 92–93, 99, 103,
    109–110, 141n8, 144–45n20
Silverman, Kaja, 49–50, 139n12
Smith, Valerie, 93–94, 107
Spillers, Hortense, x, 2, 3, 18, 92–96,
    96–97, 98, 146n13
Spivak, Gayatri Chakravorty, 93–94,
    96–99, 100
Sprengnether, Madelon, 146n14
Stansell, Christine, 47, 146n13

Stein, Gertrude, 5, 135nn10,11
Steptoe, Patrick, 116
Stowe, Harriet Beecher, xii, 47, 55–60
Subaltern Studies, 96–98

The Terminator, 147n23
thirtysomething, ix

Warner, Susan, 84
Warren, Mercy Otis, 27
Wheatley, Phillis, 18
Williams, Linda, 25

Young, Iris Marion, 136n23, 137n29

EVA CHERNIAVSKY is Assistant Professor of English and adjunct faculty in Women's Studies at Indiana University. Her articles have appeared in *Arizona Quarterly, Genders,* and *Discovering Difference: Contemporary Essays in American Culture.*